NATl
AMERICAN
STORYTELLING

Sept/Oct
2004

NATIVE AMERICAN
STORYTELLING
A Reader of Myths and Legends

Edited by

Karl Kroeber

Blackwell
Publishing

Editorial material and organization © 2004 by Blackwell Publishing Ltd

BLACKWELL PUBLISHING
350 Main Street, Malden, MA 02148-5020, USA
108 Cowley Road, Oxford OX4 1JF, UK
550 Swanston Street, Carlton, Victoria 3053, Australia

The right of Karl Kroeber to be identified as the Author of the Editorial Material in this Work has been asserted in accordance with the UK Copyright, Designs, and Patents Act 1988.

First published 2004 by Blackwell Publishing Ltd

Library of Congress Cataloging-in-Publication Data
Native American storytelling : a reader of myths and legends / [edited] by Karl Kroeber.
p. cm.
Includes bibliographical references and index.
ISBN 1-4051-1541-6 (hardcover : alk. paper) – ISBN 1-4051-1542-4 (pbk. : alk. paper)
1. Indians of North America–Folklore. 2. Indian mythology–North America. 3. Oral tradition–North America. 4. Storytelling–North America. I. Kroeber, Karl, 1926-

E98.F6N386 2004
398.2'089'97–dc22
2003025565

A catalogue record for this title is available from the British Library.

Set in 10/12.5 pt Dante
by Kolam Information Services Pvt. Ltd, Pondicherry, India
Printed and bound in the United Kingdom
by MPG Books Ltd, Bodmin, Cornwall

The publisher's policy is to use permanent paper from mills that operate a sustainable forestry policy, and which has been manufactured from pulp processed using acid-free and elementary chlorine-free practices. Furthermore, the publisher ensures that the text paper and cover board used have met acceptable environmental accreditation standards.

For further information on
Blackwell Publishing, visit our website:
http://www.blackwellpublishing.com

CONTENTS

Origins

FIGURES

TO THE READER

Be warned – you will have difficulty understanding the Native American stories in this collection. They are told in a fashion contrary to what you expect, since our idea of a good narrative is one filled with suspense: what will happen next? Suspense is of no importance in these tales. The form of American Indian storytelling is entirely different from the form of our storytelling. One reason for the radical difference is that all the North American Indians developed their cultures without writing. In an oral culture (a life in which nothing is written – today almost impossible to imagine) storytelling is enormously important and serves many complex and subtle but always practical functions. An Indian story is not just an airport time-killer.

Ah, you may think – myths. Many of the stories in this collection are indeed myths, but your conception of what myths are and what practical functions they served for Native Americans is probably wrong – especially if you have read or seen on television popular descriptions of "primitive myths" by "experts" like Mircea Eliade or Joseph Campbell, or some more recent and less famous pundits peddling misinformation through terms like "universal symbol" or "archetype."

Your best chance of enjoying this book is to not worry about "myth" at all and concentrate on why Native American stories are so weirdly different from our stories. The culture of a society that does not use writing, where most culture does not exist until someone speaks, is very largely constituted by storytelling. This is one reason Indians tell their stories over and over again. Several of the narratives in this collection we know were being told more than 400 years ago, many probably originated centuries before that, and all of them are certainly more than a century old (although some, like the Hopi story of the deadly hide-and-seek game, are still being told to this day). Stories that had been retold for years, decades, even generations were familiar to everyone but the youngest children. Since Native American cultures did not favor professional storytellers, and everyone told stories, listeners to a story might well have told that story themselves, perhaps many times. So suspense, passive curiosity as to what happens next, was of little interest to any Indian.

American Indian storytelling is somewhat like our performing of and listening to music. The man who buys a ticket to a performance of, say, Beethoven's Fifth Symphony is hoping to hear familiar sounds. His knowledge of this symphony and other works by Beethoven enables him to appreciate deeply the special qualities of the unique performance he pays to hear. An Indian listening to a familiar story was in an analogous position (but didn't pay), with the difference, first, that he himself was likely to have been a recitalist. Indian stories were performed for performers. And the story, of course, was constructed of words, not just sounds (although not infrequently the sound of words contributed significantly to the narrative effect, as rarely happens in our printed stories). The Indian audience listened very carefully to each teller's particular vocal inflections, verbal innovations, rhetorical omissions and additions, shifts in the order of events, modifications of character, and so forth, because these performative qualities endowed the old story with its special *contemporary* relevance. Alterations usually made the story particularly applicable to current circumstances, community issues, familial difficulties, new ideas about traditional practices. Perhaps one member of the tribal group was causing difficulties; somebody would tell an old story about a character who caused the same sort of trouble for his group. Everyone knew who, as Indians say, "the arrow of the story was pointed at" (including the target); communal pressure was exerted without openly embarrassing the trouble-maker or his relatives. And, most important, the criticism came in a form that enabled everyone by an act of individual imagination to participate in a group reaffirmation of the wisdom and usefulness of traditional culture.

This is one simple example of how old stories always entered into contemporary life – many Native Americans have testified to the powerful personal effect of stories as arrows. Other functions were subtler and more complex. Frequently a retelling was a response to another recent retelling, with modifications of details and shifts in plot emphasis being understood by the audience as a rebuttal or challenge that might suggest a different fashion of applying traditional ideas to immediate circumstances. Storytelling was a recognized way of "debating" solutions to practical personal, social, and political contemporary problems.

Native Americans were necessarily very practical people. For most of them, sheer physical survival was not easy. And all of them were acutely aware that the natural world is continually changing and that it constantly required of them new ways of adapting to it. Hunting and gathering played a significant role in every one of the more than 400 cultures in Native North America, so the Indians were always moving about, and encountering peoples with entirely different languages and customs, sometimes belligerently hostile. Indians did not sit around telling traditional stories because they were archetypal. Some stories were told for amusement and relaxation, but a majority were active applications of tribal historical experience to specific current issues, communal as well as individual. Storytelling served to enable the group to evaluate whether old procedures and ideas were still the most effective, or needed to be altered to suit new circumstances.

You cannot appreciate the stories in this volume unless you recognize that they are constructed as they are because their aim is not simply to preserve rigid traditions. Their purpose is to subject cultural practices – *and the psychological and social forces that created them* – to careful scrutiny to assess whether or not institutionalized practices need to be revised or can be reaffirmed. The great age of the stories means they are the result of many reworkings and refinements. These reshapings sharpened the efficacy of the storytelling evaluations, assuring the stories' historical wisdom was not dogmatic but dynamic. The stories had been shaped by their function as a means for uncontroversially examining against particular new conditions psychological and social tensions and pressures that had led to the institution of specific social practices. These practices embodied deeply cherished beliefs and firmly established patterns of behavior because they had worked effectively. Were they as a reliable as ever, or did unprecedented circumstances suggest modifications to sustain their efficaciousness?

Indian stories, including myths, endured for generations by continually being reconfigured. These retellings resulted in a slow, careful refining through the imaginativeness and verbal skills of many tellers. Constantly revised, the stories became more dense, more subtle, their form gradually perfected to an economical sharpness like a well-flaked arrow point – with every word and sentence contributing to an increasingly complex and nuanced meaningfulness. These stories could serve as instruments of social readjustment because their form, their artistry, had taken shape through a history of constant engagement with practical necessities. An insuperable obstacle to our appreciation of Native American storytelling is that we encounter each tale only once, in a single form. Other tellings, other performances, unknown to us, always influenced the Indian audience's understanding of a specific retelling of a tale. Despite our lack of knowledge of this *internal history* of each narrative, its careful reworkings over time, endowing it with artistic form, offer some insight into its potency as a useful, self-reflexive constituent of the dynamics of a Native American society.

Every story ever told, whether an account of something that truly happened or a fairy tale, whether printed or orally recited, articulates an act of imagination by the teller – and the story is understood by its audience through an equivalent exercise of imagination. By learning to understand the artistic form of a story, its imaginative structure, we can discover something of its deepest meaning and identify some of its probable effects on its original audiences. This is the process we use in learning to appreciate the *Odyssey*, for example, which was created in a culture that vanished three thousand years ago, and of which we have very little knowledge except what we can deduce from the Homeric epics. We use the same process, usually with more consciousness of its difficulties, when we undertake the study of a foreign literature – say, Japanese Kabuki theater. Of course, the more we can learn about the different or extinct culture the better, but finally, the depth and cogency of our understanding of the work of an alien literature depends most of all on the sensitivity we can develop to the imaginative configuring of its language – its artistic form.

The problems posed by Indian stories to this process are formidable. There were more than four hundred distinct cultures, with as many separate languages, in aboriginal North America. Because of the genocidal fury of the European invasion of the American continent, many of these cultures were totally destroyed, and all were severely ravaged. What information we have about them is thanks to a tiny band of "salvage anthropologists" who, at the beginning of the twentieth century, undertook an unprecedented program of saving and recording all aspects of the cultures that remained, often collecting information and stories from literally the last survivor of a culture and last speaker of a now extinct language. To this was added the heroic efforts of the Indians themselves, who in the last seventy years have worked assiduously against terrific obstacles, political and economic, to revive their diverse cultural heritages. Given this situation it is impossible for a non-specialist to have much knowledge of the cultural context out of which the various Indian narratives in this collection emerged. And here Alexander Pope's caution is particularly appropriate – "a little learning is a dangerous thing." Having taught this material for many years at Columbia University, I am painfully aware how much false information and how many misconceptions about American Indians are abroad. For non-specialists, the best way to gain valid insight into the mindsets of diverse Indian peoples is through understanding of the imaginative processes revealed by stories that in fact largely created and sustained their cultures.

Trouble is, this is hard work. It's easier to let some "expert" tell you what to think about Native Americans. One has to begin by disabling ingrained preconceptions about what makes a "good" story. In Indian stories plot often serves mainly to bring into meaningful contrast parallel actions, scenes, characters, and speeches that have no direct causal connection. This large rhetorical structure is supported by a preference for paratactic sentences. Where we are likely to say "Because it becomes cold, bears hibernate," the paratactic Indian style is "Bears hibernate. It snows." Our style is to connect the two parts of the sentence with an unequivocal cause–effect relation, a relation often made equivocal in Indian stories. It is not that Indians necessarily believe that bears hibernating cause winter, but they are more modest than we in assuming they infallibly know what causes things to happen. Generally, the Indians found their world more complicated, uncertain, and changeable than we do ours. The paratactic style leaves more to listeners' imaginations – they are not *told* what the relation of two events is; they are encouraged to imagine different possibilities and implications of the relationship.

Analogously, we are likely to encounter late in a Native American story a character who seemingly has no connection with any other characters. If we examine what happens to the new character, what he does or thinks, we will probably see that in some way his circumstances or actions parallel that of a character we have met earlier, and in some way presents a dramatic contrast. This contrastive parallelism is what Native American tellers and listeners concentrated on – in such similarities and differences the deepest meanings of the stories are embodied. The Indian teller evokes his listeners' freedom to imagine. The teller does not trace out explicit connections; he provokes listeners to conceive of these. He is not telling a story he privately invented but one that belongs to his people, one that has been told before and will be told again by others. Indians valued excellent recitalists, especially if they were inventive and innovative. But tellers and audience sought new meanings in old stories. Indian tellers did not "express" their subjective feelings; they exerted their talents in the service of stories worth telling because they sustained the health of their community.

Indian storytelling depends on more active imaginative participation in the story by the audience than is asked by our fiction. If you are more than twelve years old and an admirer of the Harry Potter books you will probably not enjoy these Indian narratives, because they require vigorous *independence* of imaginative response from each member of their audience, helping each to become more useful to the community. The Harry Potter books are very easy to read because they encourage us to be passive, to let somebody else imagine for us by staying within entirely expected patterns of fantasy, the commodified imagery that characterizes most popular contemporary fiction. Our "fantasy" is tame, pallid, and unspectacular compared to what we find in the Native American narratives, in which anything can happen: a woman with a hole in the top of her head into which she reaches to take out some brains to drop them in the food she is preparing; an old man with a penis thirty feet long; a girl who eats her own body, a talking fly, an heroic protagonist whose name is Placed-Next-to-Testicles, a giant who smashes mountains with his fist. Perhaps even more upsetting than the open sexuality of the Indian stories or their talking animals are the major characters who appear simultaneously as a human being and an animal.

I observed that American Indians were of necessity very practical peoples whose physical survival was often in jeopardy. They delighted in jokes and funny tales, but many of their stories dealt with very serious social, moral, environmental, and psychological problems central to their immediate well-being. The weird, exaggerated, violent, impossible features of their narratives were not escapist fantasizing, but their means for imagining very real (often very common) situations, feelings, attitudes, beliefs of the utmost importance to the functioning of their societies. They thought of storytelling as a strenuous imaginative exercise. Their storytelling never wasted time with superficial verisimilitude, like our "realistic" fiction, because Indian cultures were principally constructed by storytelling. Indian stories were intended to highlight and evaluate the deepest personal emotions and the most fundamental social structures that allowed a community to function productively and enduringly. The violent exaggerations and impossibilities with which their stories abound are means for arousing heightened awareness of private feelings that few of us ever express publicly, or of fundamental patterns of social behavior and moral commitments that are so much the bedrock of daily behavior that their validity is taken for granted and never critically examined. What seem to us absurdities are dramatizing modes to enable Indian listeners to explore in their minds the most essential and sacred principles of the institutions upon which their society is founded and depends for its successful continuance.

For us, stories are usually light entertainment, trivial amusements, with which we while away – waste – time. For Indians, storytelling was their most important cultural activity. Every one of their most sacred rituals was rooted in a narrative. Storytelling articulated the foundational systems and commitments by which each unique cultural life was formed, and at the same time it was the primary means by which those systems and commitments could be examined so as to be better understood, sustained, modified, and improved. Their narratives seem to us strange because they are far more culturally serious than the stories we read and watch on television, and they demand far more daring, adventurous, and ultimately responsible imagining that we are trained to bring to our story responses. We cannot begin to comprehend the power of these narratives until we recognize that nothing that is strange or exaggerated in them is told simply for superficial effect (or in the service of such nonsense as "universal symbolism"). Read as Indians heard them, these stories are troubling (and exciting) because they make manifest the deepest psychological or sociological forces that determined the nature of the lives of tellers and audiences, forces which, except for the stories, would have remained unacknowledged and unexamined – and therefore potentially disruptive and destructive.

Two fundamental conceptions of Native Americans that are determinative of the form and substance of their narratives must be emphasized, because they are so antithetical to our habitual ways of thinking. Whereas we regard individuality as the result of idiosyncratic subjective traits that distinguish one person from everyone else, Indians conceived of individuality as established by the special intensity with which a person embodied and practiced the essential characteristics of his or her culture. They did not disassociate individuality from culture, as against our view of individuality as a meta-cultural independence. For them, the uniqueness of a person, a Navajo, say, could be realized only by the person thinking and acting in a fashion distinct from the way any person from a non-Navajo culture would think, feel, and act. In their stories, consequently, little attention is given to details of idiosyncratic subjectivity, while much is focused on individualization established through communal interdependence.

Interdependence also defines the Indians' sense of their world and their place in it. Our Judeo-Christian tradition absolutely separates the natural from the supernatural; for Native Americans the natural environment is in every aspect divine in its naturalness. The physical world in which all humans dwell is sacred because every part of it, from the tiniest insect to the cosmic whole, from grubworms to the constellation of stars forming the Great Bear, from giant redwoods to dandelions, is equally infused with divine life and equally worthy of respect for what it is in itself and as a useful contributor to the dynamism of the whole.

Our monotheistic traditions make it difficult for us to understand this conception of what might be called ecological sacredness, a view that enabled Indians to find absolutely everything in the world both interesting and valuable. In the hundreds of Indian stories I have studied, I have never encountered a single case of ennui. We must try to enter their mindset of eager attention to one's surroundings if we are appreciate that Indian sacred stories are exploratory rather than doctrinal. Myths characteristically are dramatic investigations into the underlying personal and communal tensions that gave rise to the establishment of particular social institutions. Indian myths are practically useful because they are dynamically evaluative, not merely dogmatic. Storytelling was the principal means by which Native Americans sustained and strengthened, through continual self-reflexive reassessments, the effectiveness of their cultures in a world sacred because vital – never static nor dependably stable, yet therefore hospitable to beings capable of self-transformation and self-renewal.

A final caution on how these narratives may mislead. Many Native American stories are much longer than any in this collection. A great many took five to six hours to tell, and some were even longer. Our impatience with such narratives enfeebles our understanding of all Indian storytelling. Critical attention to the subject in the twentieth century has – understandably – concentrated on brief narratives. But unless we can comprehend people happy to listen through most of the night to stories repetitive in structure and with no unfamiliar plot elements, we will not grasp how and why they also created dramatically and subtly constructed shorter narratives. The very, very long stories of these oral cultures testify to the utter foreignness to us of the social function of all their narratives. Indians listened as we cannot to old legends with the kind of courtesy we give to family members and neighbors when they come to speak to us of matters seriously concerning them.

There were traditional Native American stories of heroic action. My father, Alfred Kroeber, a century ago recorded a Mojave narrative of political usurpation, exile, and revenge that can remind Westerners of Homeric epics. But such a story is, I believe, atypical. Native American longer narratives may show the world to be dangerous and that aggressive actions are sometimes required, but they tend to emphasize that human activities are more productive when adapted to the more extended and encompassing rhythms of natural life. Long stories tend to be meditative, deliberately unexciting, encouraging of careful rumination about permanently important features of the world and evoking satisfaction with a culture constructed in congruence with its processes. This does not imply simple complacency. All Indian stories facilitate community members' reasoning together about problems that lack easy solutions. But Indians were proud of their cultures as enabling them to realize the fullest potential of humanness. Many of these peoples called themselves by a name which meant in essence "human being," implying that other cultures were not fully human, as the ancient Greeks called all non-Greeks barbarians. Indians also were fascinated by their language as the primary instrument of their cultural individuality. Hearing *their* words articulating the reasons for their practices was a significantly confirmatory experience, a reassurance of continuity sustained through continuous self-renewal.

Such confirmation was valuable. For as manifest in the longer as in the shorter stories is the Indian awareness that the margin of their survival is razor thin. Not being alert to tiny signals of change or variation could lead to destruction by drought, flood, famine of a long winter, enemy attack. Few of us understand that to live as fully as Native Americans did within and as part of the natural environment was to live in continuous peril. Today's Indians with justice are bitterly contemptuous of New Age "communing" with nature and the abstract sentimentalizing about the environment common among owners of environmentally destructive automobiles. Indians, always aware of their mortality and their culture's need for continuous renewal, found profit and pleasure in carefully attending to the details of everyday existence in a world both ferociously dangerous and wonderfully beneficent.

The Translations

Since the publication of an essay by the anthropological linguist Dell Hymes in 1958 in the *International Journal of American Linguistics* 24:4 (257), noting a definable formal structure of Chinook myths crucial for their meanings, anthropologists concerned with the aboriginal cultures of North America have increasingly insisted that the significance of these stories cannot be divorced from the forms of their telling. Translations therefore should make apparent something of the original's formal organization, that is to say, the artistry with which they were constructed in their telling. This led to a now common practice pioneered by Dennis Tedlock of printing translations in typographical forms indicative of the contours of an actual oral performance: punctuation, lineation, and different typefaces are used to represent pauses in delivery, raising or lowering of the voice, differences in speed of delivery, and so forth. While appropriate for stories mechanically recorded, this method is inapplicable to the vast number of tellings recorded in the past only by the ethnologist's pencil. Furthermore, no one has yet unmistakably identified distinctive formal characteristics of any Indian culture's style of storytelling. This is not an easy task for us, because none of the Native American cultures made use of the formal devices of Western literatures, metrical patterning, rhymes, and the like; Indian stories even employ metaphor sparingly. Larger rhetorical structuring poses equivalent problems. Our stories aim for closure. Indians preferred open-endedness. They expected and wanted stories retold: what mattered was the continuing vitality of their culture. Indian tellers always disclaimed originality, insisting even when they were obviously innovative and creative that they only recited a narrative heard or dreamed by someone before them. Indian storytellers expunged the subjectivity our contemporary writers often give precedence over narrative.

This situation is frustrating for scholars, but not surprising. Forty-five years is little time in which to gain insight into what is in fact a truly – not superficially – alien form of storytelling, even though it sometimes looks deceptively similar to our own. In more than a century we have not advanced very far in our understanding of the art of prehistoric cave-paintings, although no one who has looked at them doubts that they manifest art of a high order. As I've pointed out, the artfulness of Native American stories is commonly the product of perhaps hundreds of retellings, over the course of decades, perhaps centuries. This is a communal art dependent on slow, complex, cumulative processes calling forth the imaginativeness and verbal adroitness of many performers self-consciously retelling in changing circumstances. We as yet know very little about these storytelling traditions. There is, for example, to date only one systematically detailed comparative analysis of differences in tellings of the same story by two Indians using the same language. Until detailed comparative analyses like this are multiplied many times we cannot expect to identify artistic conventions utilized by individual Native American storytellers – and remember, in native North America there were, literally, hundreds of distinct languages and cultures. In these circumstances, our most important responsibility is so far as possible not to impose our preconceptions of form and purpose on narratives from peoples whose social, intellectual, and religious traditions radically differed – and continue to differ – from ours.

Translations are always inadequate, but they can be exceedingly valuable, as Keats claimed in his famous sonnet on reading Homer in Chapman's translation. Ancient Greek literature is still a significant aesthetic and intellectual force in our culture today – witness Derek Walcott's *Omeros*. But the truth is that few of us, including Walcott, are fluent in classical Greek. One failure of all translations of Indian stories, however, especially bothers me. The more I have studied the narratives, the more I have come to realize that the best stories carried, along with their social and psychological insights and their spiritual wisdom, terrific emotional impact. I begin to discern faintly through the printed text the effect, for example, of a favored Indian rhetoric of repetition, that, if heard recited aloud, hammering in one's ears, would build up an almost intolerable pressure of feeling. Although this dimension of the stories is almost entirely lost in the texts I present, what is missing may be hinted at in the following excerpt from a recording made by my father a century ago, of a Yurok woman's recitation in which the translation attempts to reproduce as faithfully as possible the manner of her telling. It is a story (unfortunately never recorded completely) of obsession, and to me even the English phrases enforce the terror and fascination of obsessional feeling. Try reading the passage aloud – the right way to read all these stories.

YUROK *That is where he lived, he that played the flute: at Espeu, that is where he lived, he that played the flute. All at once he thought, "Now I shall learn to play," and he used to make music all day. Then he would go for sweat-house wood, after he had finished playing, and then play at night. He did not sleep; he played the flute constantly. All at once he thought, "I shall do that." In the day he used to go to Plek'en and to Neges and cry.*

He was the father of a child, of one child. And he had a wife, but suddenly he paid no more attention to her, for he had decided to play, and had made a flute – not the sort of flute they have now, but the flute of long ago, the kind Indians used to play. And he used to play on this until far in the night; some nights he did not sleep at all, he played so long, and from the house she would hear him, his wife. The playing seemed so near and she could hear him so plainly, the playing seemed so near and she could hear him so plainly, that she thought, "What makes him like that?" His wife thought this, the playing seemed so near and she could hear him so plainly. Their child was a little girl. But he paid no attention to his wife, and began to play, and as soon as day broke started to get sweat-house wood, and would go to Neges and to Plek'en, crying.

So he did that, playing the flute: every night he played, every night he played. He used not to sleep, but played continually; he would play and then cry. He thought, "I will do thus." He longed for he did not know what, and used to think, "What am I longing for?" All day and all night until morning he would cry and play the flute, such as they used to have, not the kind they have now, but the flute that the Indians used to play on, on that he played. In the morning he would lay down his flute and go for sweat-house wood, he would always do the same: he would go from crag to crag to Espeu, and to Neges, and sit and think of many things. He did not at all want to see his wife. Their child was a little girl, but he no longer noticed her: all he did was to play. He played until morning and cried, longing for he did not know what. He would say, "I do not know what I am longing for."

[A. L. Kroeber, "He Who Swam Across the Ocean," *Yurok Myths.* Berkeley: University of California Press (1976), 453–4.]

In this volume I use the earliest translations by linguists and anthropologists, which were usually made in the simplest form of direct transcription unaccompanied by commentary on the form of the narratives. I have made minor adjustments in punctuation, diction, and phrase order for clarity only where English usages of a century ago have become obscure or disconcertingly quaint – modifications that will be readily apparent to anyone consulting the original texts. I have given at least minimal representation to all the major North American culture areas, and included multiple examples of the two major ethnographic narrative categories, "origin myths" and "trickster tales" (Stories 6–9 and 13–16 respectively).

But principally I have selected stories that seem to me to manifest especially skillful Indian storytelling and are particularly illuminating of Indian foci of interest, special rhetorical techniques, and social/psychological purposes in telling stories. It should be remembered how tiny this sampling is: besides the hundred of Native American narratives now in print, there are thousands more unprinted, preserved in manuscripts and notebooks in libraries and museums across the United States. And of course, living Indians today continue to tell and retell stories.

I have deliberately refrained from offering any but the most essential ethnological background to the narratives. Such information is plentiful and easily available: the volumes of the *Handbook of American Indians* under the general editorship of William Sturdevant, issued by the Smithsonian Institution in Washington, DC, provide vast amounts of information based on the most recent scholarship. Almost every existent Indian culture now has its own website on the internet providing steadily increasing information both about their current life and their ancient traditions. But I hope that, instead of lazily expecting somebody else to explain Indian stories for you, that you will be provoked into exercising your own imagination to enter into the imaginings of people whose daily lives were very different from yours, but who often confronted psychological, familial, and social problems that still make our lives difficult. I encourage you to make up your own mind by having eliminated the usual story titles. Orally told stories do not have titles in our sense, and those applied by collectors, usually non-Indians, I find dangerously misleading. Contemporary readers are so habituated to taking other people's directions seriously that a title given to a traditional Indian narrative concentrates attention on what is often, from the Indian point of view, a trivial part of the story. A gambler couldn't find a safer bet than that an Indian tale entitled "Why the Buffalo has Horns" or "How it Happens that Rivers Run Downhill" is only peripherally concerned with, respectively, buffalo and rivers. The title, remember, was supplied by an ethnographer who may not have understood the story any better than you do on first reading.

I believe passionately, however, that these translations offer readers who have the courage to tackle their unconventionality and mind-boggling differences from our way of storytelling some wonderfully refreshing and genuinely thought-provoking experiences. I would suggest, for example, that seldom in our literature does one find the kind of subtlety and sensitivity to nuances of gender relations developed in many Native American stories. But a passionate person is a prejudiced one, so I'd suggest your begin by skipping my headnotes and reading the story first, perhaps two or three times. Then look at my notes (which in every case omit several dozen comments that ought to be made to elucidate the excellence of the telling), which I hope will make your next rereading more rewarding. My personal experience is that at about the tenth rereading I feel I am just beginning to get the hang of the narrative's richer implications. But my personal payoff for these rereadings has been fantastically rich. I have gained understandings of social, psychological, and moral realities fully as valuable as those I have acquired from the best of our literature, which I have been lucky enough to spend most of my life reading and teaching. The very strangeness of the Indian materials has given me refreshing new perspectives on my own culture and its stories, and I hope this collection will offer you equivalent rewards.

TEWA

Native Americans believed that a mask does not disguise, but reveals. It reveals true inner characteristics of its wearer. For Indians, masks were living artifacts. Wearing a mask affected the wearer, even as the mask was affected by the wearer. To put on a mask was not merely to impersonate: it was to become the being the mask both represented and was – and thereby to manifest part of one's self. Our difficulty in recognizing the complex personal and social implications of Indian masking is exacerbated by our not living as the Indians did in small communities threatened by harsh environmental conditions. These demanded loyalty to social conventions but also self-reliance, especially a readiness to assume personal responsibility at moments of crisis. In the conduct of ordinary daily life it was most efficient for a small group to allot labor according to gender. In some tribes women were responsible for farming work, in others men; in some tribes men did the weaving, in others women. But the scarcity of human resources made it equally essential to have institutionalized means for making use of the special talents of any individual, whatever their gender or psychological idiosyncrasies. A large number of Indian stories focus on the anomalies created by disjunctions between communal necessities and personal inclinations.

The protagonist of this story begins rebelliously. Laughing Warrior Girl rejects the authority of male elders to force her into a conventional female role. Yet when the community is attacked, and her uncle wants her to prove the validity of her claim to transcend gender limitations, he must seek for her among the other women doing women's work. She has rebelled without abandoning her social responsibilities. So she responds to her uncle's challenge gaily, laughing and singing a war song, carrying her musical instrument along with mens' weapons to battle, and taunting the enemy by flaunting her sex. As she fights victoriously her face transforms into a warrior mask, a

Figure 1   Tlingit mask. This haunting Tlingit shaman's mask suggests why masks were so important in different ways to a variety of Native American cultures. The mask climaxes a flow of power from sacred natural forces through an individual into a visible manifestation of spiritual energy. Story 23 fo Ga-Nus-Quah and the origin of Onondaga mask-making narratively embodies this circular flow of power. The divided Tlingit face-mask also suggests the unification of dual sexual forces attained by Laughing Warrior Girl to the benefit of all here people in the Tewa story 1.

("Tlinget Shaman's Mask," #330968, Photographer Rota, reproduced by permission of the Department of Library Services of the American Museum of Natural History.)

public manifestation of her personal fulfillment. But when chosen war chief, she acts as a "good girl." As with the mask, the story dramatizes her behavior as an adapting of social tradition to distinctive subjectivity. This is why Laughing Warrior Girl can sustain her community both as warrior and as healer. The bequeathing of her mask to her descendants confirms that to be a genuinely "good" Tewa one must keep alive a dynamic interplay between features of individuality such as temperament and gender and the demands of social institutions. A majority of Native American stories address this paradox – that only in the affirmation of personal independence lies the possibility of an enduringly strong community. It is notable that nearly half the narratives in this collection begin with some equivalent of the Tewa "Where they lived, lived Laughing

Warrior Girl." *This grounds the story as one of a community of others by the same people (*"*they*"*) with an established, ongoing life, into which breaks the unusual individual.*

1
From Elsie Clews Parsons, *Tewa Tales*. Washington, DC: Memoirs of the American Folklore Society, 19 (1926), 191–2.

Where they were living lived Laughing Warrior Girl, a girl who would not mind her mother or father or uncle. They were telling her to be a good girl, but she got angry quickly. Then they got tired telling her to be good so they just let her go. One time she was grinding corn, and many enemies were coming, very close to the village. Her uncle came to her house and asked her mother where she was. Her mother said she was grinding corn. He went to where she was grinding and caught her arm and said, "Take your bow and arrows and go and fight with the enemies who are coming. You would not mind us and behaved like a boy. Now is the time for you to go and fight and be brave," said the uncle to the girl. She laughed ha! ha! "I am very glad to go," she said. "I am very anxious to go and fight the enemies. I am not afraid. I will do all I can." – "That is why I tell you. Come out!" said the uncle. "I will," she said. She stood up and her uncle gave her bow and arrows and hung the bandolier around her. Then she looked around and there was a rattle hanging on the wall. She stepped up and got it. Then she started to sing. As soon as she stopped singing, she laughed ha! ha! She sang four times in the room. Then she went out and sang outdoors four times. Whenever she paused in singing she laughed ha! ha! because she was not afraid to fight. Then she started, and the men followed her. People were saying, "The Cottonwood People (clan) girl (*te'towa*) is going to fight." Some of them laughed at her. But she just went on, singing and laughing ha! ha! happy she was going to fight. Before she met the enemies, she pulled her dress up, four times, to show the enemies that she was a girl.

Then she fought. She killed all the enemies that same day. After that the fighting was over and she turned back. The men fighting with her saw she had turned *okuwa*: she was wearing a mask, one side was blue, and one side was yellow, and she had long teeth. They were afraid of her, she looked strange, she no longer looked like a girl. But she kept on singing her song, ending with ha! ha! She kept on going home, and the men followed her. When they got to the village, all the people came out and watched the girl, how she had become some sort of a person. When she went to war, she did not look like that. She went to her house and went in, and then she took off her mask and hung it on the wall, and she hung her rattle in the same place and the bow and arrow close, too. That is the way that girl became Laughing Warrior Girl. Her uncles came to the house at night. They had been talking about her. All day they had been thinking that she must be a man. So they went in there, all gathered together, the oldest uncle said they would put her in as Pota'i (war chief). Even if she was a girl, she was a man, too. So they said that whenever enemies came she was to be the leader in war. "You have to watch for the people," they told her. "If any sickness comes, you have to drive the sickness away from the people. And consider that the people are all your children. Treat them right," they told her. After that she became a good girl, she no longer acted as she used to. When war came, she went first and dressed as she did before in war. After she died, she left her mask and said that it would represent her. She would always be with the people, even if dead. "I will be with you all the time," she said, "the mask is me," she said. That is why those Cottonwood People keep that mask.

KALISPELL[1]

*This story uses a Kalispell pronoun form for which there is no English equivalent.
Linguists call this an "object-focus-form"; it identifies the person referred to as the
significant agent of an action even when not grammatically the sentence subject. It is as
if in English we could substitute "hem" for "him" in the sentence, "The arrow struck
hem in the shoulder," to indicate that the man shot was nevertheless the most
important person in the action. Many Indian languages possess analogous linguistic
characteristics that are not part of English, nor any Indo-European language. This
makes translation hideously difficult. In this story, for instance, the object-focus-form is
skillfully used as a rhetorical device to reinforce the psychological and moral superiority
of the threatened young man Rabbit to both convention-bound women and the bully
Thunder. It also is used to develop the theme of compassion, imagining oneself in the
position, physical, social, psychological, of another, a central motif in a great many
Native American stories. Here a young protagonist pities his age-afflicted grandmother,
announces his intention of finding her a helper, and does so by kidnaping another man's
wife for himself. Young Rabbit says what he is going to do and then does it. Speech
shapes reality for the socially responsible person. His chosen wife is afraid for his life,
but his assurance never wavers. Her companions resist his violation of convention as
fruitlessly as Thunder with his noisily ineffective assault. The youth frightens the
blustering bully by looking him coolly in the eye, proving himself the better man –
and therefore the better husband. Had Thunder behaved with sensible courtesy by*

1 A translation of this story showing the importance of the deployment of object-focus-form
pronouns to its formal organization is presented by Paul D. Kroeber in "Rhetorical Structure
of a Kalispell Narrative," *Anthropological Linguistics* 37:2 (1995), 119–40.

speaking before acting, he would not have lost, nor deserved to lose, his wife. Conventions (such as marriage) that give essential structure to communal life possess meaningful reality only when sustained by strong personal feeling expressed by unequivocal speech and behavior. Fearlessly saying what we mean and behaving exactly as we say we will assure the productive balance by which individual desires truly fulfill the purposes of social institutions – even when fundamental regulations appear to be violated.

2
From Evon Vogt, *The Kalispell Language: An Outline of the Grammar with Texts, Translations, and Dictionary.* Oslo: Det Norske Videnskaps-Akademi (1920), 28.

A young man (Rabbit) lived with his grandmother. One day he pitied her, because she had become old. He told her, "I will go." The next morning he got ready, and he then told his grandmother, "I will fetch someone to be your helper in the future."

Then the young man walked away. He came to an open field where women were gathering camas bulbs.[2] The young man sat down. While they were digging, he looked around, and he noticed someone, and he said, "That one, the one in the red shirt, will be my wife."

Then he went among the many working women, and approached the woman in the red shirt. She spoke to him, saying, "Oh, so you are walking around here?" He told her, "Yes, I am here to fetch you; you will be my wife."

Her companions were watching them, and they asked her, "What is that young man saying to you?" She answered, "He tells me, 'I am here to fetch you; you will be my wife.'"

The woman's companions laughed. They laughed at the young man. They said to her, "Follow him for a little while, and then turn back." So she followed him for a little while, and her friends said to her, "Do you really believe him and plan to go home with him?" They told her, "You had better turn back now."

But then the young man grabbed the woman, and he grabbed her tight. The other women went up to him, and tried to pull his hands off her. He said, "I will not let you go; I say you will be my wife."

She told him, "No, I have a husband, a man-eater." The young man said to her, "Who is your husband?"

---

2 Wild edible bulbs that were a major food source for Indians in the Northwest.

She told him, "Thunder is already my husband." He laughed at her: "You do not have a husband." She told him, "No, you will be killed." He told her, "You do not have a husband."

One of the other women stood well apart from them. The young man started to hold red-shirt even tighter. She told him, "Now you let me go, you might be killed." He told her, "No," and again, "You do not have a husband."

Then the other woman standing a ways off said, "*Pppuwa. pppuwa.*" "Look, you are already being told on," and as the woman finished speaking, *witseen, witseen* and the sky darkened. Then she told him, "Look – that is my husband." Oh, he laughed and he said, "You do not have a husband."

Then suddenly over their heads Thunder roared. She told him, "Now, please, let me go; you might get killed." "I will not let you go, because you are going to be my wife."

Thunder rushed upon Rabbit. As he came close, Rabbit looked up and opened his eyes wide. Thunder stopped, afraid of him. Thunder turned around and then rushed at him again. As he came close the young man looked up, and opened his eyes wide, and Thunder was afraid of him.

Thunder stopped still, and said to the young man, "Pity me; give me back my wife." "Had you asked at once for pity I would have given her back to you." Then Thunder said, "I love her; you must give her back to me." Then the young man answered, "Ha! perhaps I also love her."

KATHLAMET

Only rarely do Indian stories concentrate attention on the subjectivity of principal characters. Protagonists often are not even named. Indian stories tell mostly of actions and their consequences, emphasizing not characters' motives but the effects of their behavior on a community. Ancient Greek and Shakespearean tragedies commonly focus on the destruction of impressive individuals: Oedipus, Hamlet, Othello. American Indian storytellers' concentration on communal effect rather than subjective psychology is sustained by a rhetoric of repetition, especially effective in oral recitation but unfamiliar and often irritating to contemporary readers. The cumulative effect of this story is built up through formulaic questions and answers enumerating most of the major Kathlamet artifacts. All of these, whether made by men or women, the chief rejects in favor of the "Shining Thing." This, because not specifically identified, suggests the brightest object in our universe, the Sun itself, which was the inspiration for the chief's long journey.

The rhetoric of pounding repetition manifests the obsessiveness of the chief's personal desire. Then the consequences of his possessiveness are driven home unsparingly when in village after village after village after village he slaughters his own people, unable to free himself from what is now the old woman's "blanket" (the term an ironic reminder that the "Shining Thing" is not something created by man or woman). This hideous possession is more fearful than the shirt of Nessus that destroyed Hercules, because the Kathlamet protagonist is not killed by it. He lives on in full consciousness that he is the sole murderer of all his family and all his people and the destroyer of all the clothes, weapons, and domestic furniture that they painstakingly made with their own hands. In my years of studying literature I have never encountered a more terrifying dramatization of the responsibilities of power and the destructiveness of ambition.

3

From Franz Boas, *Kathlamet Texts*. Washington, DC: Bulletin of the Bureau of American Ethnology 26 (1901), 26–32.

There was a chief of a town. His relatives lived in five towns. In the morning be used to go outside and stay out to look at the Sun. The Sun was about to rise. He said to his wife: "What would you think if I went to see the Sun?" His wife said to him: "Do you think he is near that you want to go there?" On the following day he went out again. Again he saw the Sun. It was nearly sunrise. He said to his wife: "Make me ten pairs of shoes. Make me ten pairs of leggings." The woman made ten pairs of shoes and ten pairs of leggings. The next morning he went. He went far away. He used up his shoes and his leggings. Then he put on another pair of shoes and leggings. He went for ten months. Then he had used five pairs of shoes and five pairs of leggings. He went for ten months. Then he was near the place where the Sun was rising and he had used all his shoes. Then he found a large house. He opened the door. There was a girl. He entered and stayed there. He saw arrows hanging on one side of the house. Quivers full of arrows were hanging there. There were hanging shirts of elk skin, wooden armor, shields, stone axes, bone clubs, and head ornaments. Implements used by men were hanging on the one side of the house. On the other side were mountain-goat blankets, dressed elkskin blankets, buffalo skins, dressed buckskins, long dentalia, shell beads, and short dentalia. Near the doorway some large thing was hanging. He did not know it. He asked the girl: "Whose are these quivers?" [She said:] "They are my father's mother's property. When I am grown up, she will give them away." "Whose are these elkskin armors?" "They belong to my father's mother. When I am grown up, she will give them away." "Whose are these arrows?" "They belong to my father's mother. When I am grown up, she will give them away." "Whose are these wooden armors?" "They belong to my father's mother. When I am grown up, she will give them away." "Whose are these shields and war clubs?" "They belong to my father's mother. When I am grown up, she will give them away." "Whose are these stone axes?" "They belong to my father's mother." Then also be asked about the things on the other side of the house: "Whose are these buffalo skins?" "They belong to my father's mother and to me. When I am grown up, she will give them away." "Whose are these mountain-goat blankets?" "They belong to my father's mother. When I am grown up, she will give them away." "Whose are these dressed buckskins?" "They belong to my father's mother. When I am grown up, she will give them away." "Whose are these deerskin blankets?" "They belong to my father's mother. When I am grown up, she will give them away." "Whose are these shell beads?" "They belong to my father's mother. When I am grown up, she will give them away." "Whose are these long dentalia?" "They belong to my father's mother. When I am grown up, she will give them away." "Whose are these short dentalia?" "They belong to my father's mother. When I am grown up, she will give them away."

He asked about all those things, and thought: "I will take them." When it was evening, the old woman came home. She hung up something that pleased him. It was shining. He stayed there a long time and took that girl. They remained there. Every morning the old woman disappeared. At night she came back. She brought home all kinds of things. She brought home arrows. Sometimes she brought mountain-goat blankets and elkskin shirts. She did so every day. He stayed there a long time; then he grew homesick. For two days he did not rise. She asked her granddaughter: "Did you scold him and is he angry?" "No, I did not scold him; he is homesick." Then she asked her son-in-law: "What do you wish to have when you go home? Do you want these buffalo skins?" He said: "No." "Do you want these mountain-goat blankets?" He said: "No." "Do you want these elkskin shirts?" He said: "No." She showed him all that was on the one side of the house. Next she showed him the ornaments. She showed him everything. He liked that great thing that was hanging there. When that thing turned around it was shining so that one had to close one's eyes. That he wanted. He said to his wife: "The old woman shall give me only her blanket." His wife said to him: "She will not give it to you. The people tried to buy it, but she will not give it away." Then he became angry. After some days she asked him again: "Will you take this?" She showed him everything. She showed him all the implements used by men. When she came to that thing that was hanging there, she was silent. Then she became tired and said: "Take it, but look out if you carry it. You wanted it. I wished to love you and I do love you." Then she hung it onto him and she gave him a stone ax. She said: "Now go home." Now he went home.

He did not see a town until he came near his uncle's town. Now the thing which he carried in his hands shook, and said: "We shall strike your town." Then he lost his senses, and he broke his uncle's town and killed all the people. Now he recovered. He had broken all the houses. His hands were full of blood. Then he thought: "Oh, what a fool I was! The thing I wanted is bad." He tried to throw it away, but it stuck to his flesh. Then he went. He went a short distance and again he lost his senses. He came to the town of another one of his uncles. Again the thing said: "We shall strike your town." He tried to keep quiet, but he could not do it. He tried to throw it away, but his hands closed. Then he lost his senses, and broke all the houses. He recovered and the town of his uncle was destroyed. The people lay there dead. Then he cried and tried to strip it off in the fork of a tree, but it did not come off at all. It stuck to his body.

He tried to strike what he wore on a stone, but he could not break it. Then he went on. He came near the town of another one of his uncles, and again the thing which he carried shook. "We shall strike your town," it said. Then he lost his senses. He broke the houses of his uncle's town. He destroyed his uncle's town. Then he recovered. He cried, because he made his relatives unhappy. He tried to dive in order to take it off, but it stuck to his body. He rolled himself in a thicket, and he tried to break on a stone what he wore. Then he gave it up. He cried. He went on and came to the town of another uncle. Again the thing which he carried shook: "We shall strike your town." He lost his senses. He broke all the houses and killed all the people. Then he recovered. All the people were killed, and the town was destroyed. His arms and his hands were covered with blood. He cried: "Kā! kā! kā! kā!" and tried to break what he wore on a stone, but it did not break. He tried to throw it away, but his hands closed. He went on, and he came near his own town. He tried to remain standing, but it was as if his feet were pulled toward it. Then he lost his senses and destroyed the whole town and killed his relatives. Then he recovered. The whole town was destroyed, and the ground was full of bodies. Then he cried again: "Kā! kā! kā! kā!" He bathed and tried to take off what he wore, but it stuck to his body. Sometimes he struck it against stones and thought it might get broken. Then he gave it up. He cried.

Now he looked back, and there the old woman was standing. She said to him: "I tried to love you; I tried to be kind to your people; why do you cry? You wished for it and wanted to wear my blanket." Now she took it off and left him. She went home. He stayed there; he went a short distance and built a small house.

TILLAMOOK

Fantastic impossibilities in Indian stories are introduced to enable listeners to imagine *familiar* experiences, such as disturbing tensions of ordinary family and communal life. Sore Back in the opening of this story is simultaneously a boy and a weird fish. How are we to understand this? Indian storytelling does not merely recount a sequence of events but also relates every event to others through **counter-sequential** structures of parallelism and contrast. Sore Back is derided and mutilated because he has been orphaned. He is so desperate for companionship that he accepts humiliating treatment because it allows him to associate with other boys. Furthermore, the boys escape from Wild Woman (whose lack of grandchildren contrastively parallels Sore Back's lack of parents) solely because of Sore-Back, who of course gets no credit. This all-too-common injustice is given imaginative physical form in Sore-Back's bizarre physiology.

Sore Back vanishes after the opening paragraphs, but the story is filled with characters and events that through parallelism and contrast with his situation articulate diverse forms of common familial–social difficulties. Bald Eagle's daughter is abused by her own family until she is literally turned into a mole by unfair favoritism for an adopted son. The dysfunctionality of the family of Bald Eagle (who finds a child on the shore where Wild Woman kidnaped children) is the exact opposite of the incestual disaster that destroys the foundling's parents. Mole's adopted brother later befriends a ridiculed and ostracized former suitor of his wife by restoring His-Bones-Have-Been-Sucked to communal respect as a **fisherman** – his degradation deriving from his humiliation when disguised as a fish. For the Tillamook listener, who has heard the story before, and may even have told it herself, its primary interest lies in these complex systems of paralleling contrasts that can connect His-Bones-Have-Been-Sucked all the way to Sore Back, **against** the cause–effect sequentiality of the basic narrative.

Rhetorical devices of every kind work in opposition to sequential order to stimulate the audience to imagine how mythical events offer insight into commonplace practicalities of contemporary living. It is to us "unrealistic" that Wild Woman again and again descends on the beach to seize the sleeping children, who again and again escape from her in the same fashion (note how this "unrealistic" reiteration is echoed by the later unsuccessful **killings** of Wild Woman). Indian listeners do not take such repetitions literally but as invitations, first, to imagine all the emotional, social, and moral pressures manifested in the action that is repeated, and, second, to contemplate its relevance to the circumstances of their present life. Indian stories are structured to facilitate practical **audience** imaginative activity.

The rich narrative of the amazing rise of Placed-Next-to-Testicles from a disgraceful heritage to heroic stature as generous redeemer of a failed rival also serves as a vehicle for provoking thought about familiar (but difficult to discuss openly) familial dysfunctions. Wild Woman truly desires grandchildren that she is denied by her infertility (it seems right that her violent sex with Crane produces no offspring), yet it is her curse that kills the youngsters of whom she became so fond. Placed-Next-to-Testicles achieves the power to revenge himself on the killer of his parents, but then turns that power against its source, Thunder, wifeless father of a beautiful daughter pathologically hostile to all her suitors. Having overcome this exaggeration of "natural" paternal affection, and helped poor His-Bones-Have-Been-Sucked, our hero's final act is abuse of his power in order to mutilate his father-in-law. All unhappy families are unhappy in different, but not unconnected, ways.

The story's rhetorical structuring makes inescapably vivid how every positive emotion possesses the potential for being perverted. Each violently exaggerated action is counterpointed by the parallelism of an equally violently contrasting episode. This creates a total narrative form not closed, because not aimed at closure, but open to continuous reconfiguring. Indian stories are told in order to be retold. They are shaped to allow continuous reconfiguring to accommodate motives of new tellers and historical changes in society, changes that, for example, may increase the problematics of some familial–communal circumstances and diminish others. The rhetoric of sequence contravened by anti-sequence narration, although unfamiliar to us, was an ideal form of discourse for Native American societies. It was ideal because these communities without writing continuously sought to establish dynamic connections between the wisdom founded on long years of practical experience and the new, particular difficulties of the immediate present. As Indians have repeatedly insisted to uncomprehending Europeans, only stories make possible a viable culture, one capable through constantly renewed awareness of its past of devising imaginative modes of self-transformation to meet changing conditions, both internal and external.

4

From *Nehalem Tillamook Tales*, told by Clara Pearson, recorded by Elizabeth Derr Jacobs, ed. Melville Jacobs. Corvallis: Oregon State University Press (1990), 45–58.

Wild Woman was living alone. Her husband, High Class Crane, lived upriver in his own place. Every day she would go to the beach for children. She wanted to raise some grandchildren.

There on the beach at Nehalem, many children went swimming every day. One boy had no father, no mother; his grandmother took care of him. His name was Stcheelgeelun, but the boys had given him a nickname, Sore Back. They named him that because they threw mud on him and urinated on his back until his back was all sore. The other boys were awfully mean to him. They did not treat him well because he had no father and no mother. He was some kind of a blackfish that could squirt water from the top of his head. He had a sharp fin along his back. His grandmother would tell him, "I want you to quit running with those mean boys." He would not mind, no, he liked it. They would call him, "Come on, let's go swimming." All ready! He would run. He could not be taught anything.

When the boys got through swimming, they would go lie down on the hot sand and go to sleep. Sore Back went to sleep too. He always slept on the end. Wild Woman would come along with her big soft spruce-root basket and look at those boys. "I will steal them." Then she would pick up Sore Back first, because he slept on the end, and put him in the bottom of her basket. She would continue picking them up till her basket was full. Then she would put some dry rotten wood on the top so no one could see the boys, and walk home. When she got home she would put her basket down. "Wake up! grandchildren!" She removed the rotten wood; there were never any children there. Sore Back wriggled back and forth until that fin on his back wore a hole in the bottom of the basket. Everything had fallen out except the rotten wood. There would always be just that rotten wood in the basket. Then she would feel sorry, "Oh, I lost my boys." She never found out how it happened that those boys fell out. Day after day it happened that way.

Then one day it happened that a boy and his sister lay on the end and Sore Back was the third one in the row of children. That day Wild Woman put the brother and sister in the bottom of the basket and Sore Back was on top of them. Then she filled her basket with children. She put rotten wood on top, she covered them. She arrived at home, she put her basket down. "Wake up! grandchildren!" She took out the rotten wood; there she had a girl and a boy.

Sore Back had made a hole in the side of the basket and he himself and all those children on top of him had dropped out. Just those two remained in the bottom of the basket. Oh! She was pleased. She had a boy and a girl now. They awoke, they saw, "Goodness, a strange woman." She said to them, "You are my grandchildren." Then she told them, "You go and see grandpa. Grandpa will feed you; he has quantities of little fish." They went to Crane. "Grandmother told us to come and see if grandpa would give us something to eat." "Yes," he said, "I have a lot of trout already cooked." He fed them. They ate, they returned. Ah, Wild Woman liked those children. Every morning she got ready, she took her basket, away she went traveling in the mountains. She pretended that she was going to dig roots. But she really went to get poison lizards, water dogs, and such things, and she brought a basket full of them in the afternoon. That was the time she did not want the children around. The children kept her fire for her while she was away. She would tell the children, "Do not look at me. Go to grandpa and tell him to feed you." Then she would dig in the hot ashes and she would roast those lizards there. She would say, "Up at Tillamook Mountain, I dug one. At Nestucca, I dug one." In that manner she would name all the rivers and mountains, and in each place she had dug but one. She could travel all over in an hour; she went in a different way from the way an ordinary person travels. She would tell the children, "Do not look at me. You go to grandpa and tell him to feed you." She did not want the children watching her and seeing her eating those animals. Every day she did like that.

Those children grew very rapidly. She spent a great deal of time amusing them. She gathered sea shells for the little girl to play with as dolls; and she told her husband, "You make that boy a little canoe to play with." Indeed she liked those children, but she had nothing for them to eat. She always had to tell them, "You go to grandpa. He will feed you."

At times she neglected to go for those animals. And sometimes she would get peculiar. Then she would tell those children, "Go tell grandpa to tell you a story." Those children would go, usually evenings, though may be in the afternoon once in a while. They would arrive there. "Grandmother, she said you should tell us a story." "Oh," grandpa would say, "you do not want to pay any attention to her. She talks funny sometimes. There is no story to tell." (If she wanted to make love with that old man, why didn't she go there without having him tell a story?) Then after a while grandpa would start in and tell a story to the children, and of course they did not understand what it was or why he always told the same one. He would finish and say, "There! That's all. That's a short story." They would run home then. There Wild Woman would be poking in the fire with her face turned away. "Well, did grandpa tell you a story?" "Yes, he told us a story." Then the old woman would rub her eyes and say, "Oh, that smoke got in my eyes. It is making me cry. That smoke went in my eyes. What did grandpa say?" The little girl would not tell, but the boy would, he would repeat it word for word. "Grandpa said, 'I looked down the river, and there was a small canoe down there, and there was a person paddling. He does not sit up straight, that one who paddles, he is kind of stooped over. And that canoe is not perfect, it is somewhat lopsided, that canoe!'" (She would get a little angry because he [Crane] was really talking about her.) "And grandpa said, 'After a while I looked up in the sky, and oh, that sky was all clouds, and I saw a bunch of grass growing up on that sky.'" Then Wild Woman would seem very angry. "He is always talking about my dead people!" She called it talking about a dead person so the children would think he was talking straight. Then she would get ready, put on her best shawl, and take her double-bladed knife. "I'm not going to hurt him very much," she would say, "because you children get your meals there. I'm not going to hurt him very much." When Wild Woman returned she always had scratches on her arms. She dug them with her own fingernails to make it appear to the children that she had been fighting. After she had gone, the little girl would always say, "Oh, what did you want to tell her for? Every word that grandpa said? That always makes her angry. Maybe she will go kill grandpa."

So it kept up. Sometimes she would go get her lizards and water dogs and then she would tell the children, "Go get your meal at grandpa's." But whenever she wanted it [coitus], then she wanted that story business. After a while the children were grown up. They had become smarter. They liked Wild Woman, but they liked the old man better because that was where they ate. Again she sent them for a story. After she had gone with her double-bladed knife, the girl said, "Oh, maybe she will kill him this time. Let us go and watch. What does she do to grandpa all the time?" They went, they hurried, they sneaked around where they could see through a crack. Wild Woman arrived, she said, "*Mmmmm*, you are always talking bad about my dead people." Crane said, "Aw! Do not be always talking, just keep still." Then Wild Woman received what she wanted. The children watched. "Oh, they are doing something that does not look good." Somehow they knew what it was. "Ah! She cannot be killing him since grandpa is on top." Suddenly Wild Woman realized that someone was looking at her. She said, "Let me up. Eyes are looking at me." She called outside, "I will fix you when I get hold of you." Crane would not let her up because he knew it must be his grandchildren watching, and he feared she would kill them. The children were frightened. "Let us go. She said if she got hold of us she would fix us."

They went, the girl gathered up her dolls, the boy took his bow and arrow, and they ran as they went away. The girl overlooked two of her dolls, a boy doll and a girl doll. She had not picked them all up. Their grandfather held Wild Woman as long as he was able. Finally she pulled herself away from him. She went home, she looked around. No children anywhere. After a while she went and looked in the corner where the little girl played with her dolls. She found those two that were left. "Oh, they have run away," she realized. She picked up those two dolls, the boy and the girl, she talked to those dolls. She said, "You are my grandson, and you are my granddaughter. I will cause them to do the same thing they watched me do. They are to do it before the night is past. They were looking at me, they watched me." Then she started out to follow them. Her husband followed her. That husband, Crane, he himself had [spirit] power. He made hills, "Oh, I wish everything may become a big hill, so she will be unable to get around quickly." After a while night came, Wild Woman gave it up. She went back home.

That brother and sister crossed a creek. Then they made it [magically] into a big river so it could no longer be waded. The boy got some slivers from a tree, he made a tiny house, like a real one. He put beds inside, fixed a place for the fire to be built, he put shelves in the corners, made a door, everything exactly as in a real house. When he finished he sat down by the little door of his tiny house. He put his hands together, he blew through them right into the door. Lo! He blew into that tiny house until it became a large house. He had a strong power. Then he said to his sister, "Well, we will go in and try to build a fire." He took a drill, he built a fire. Since he was the bigger, he made decisions. He told her, "That is your bed on the other side of the fire, you will stay there. I will stay on this side." After a while they went to bed. The girl got the full effect of Wild Woman's wish. She had left her two dolls. But the boy did not get any effect because he had not forgotten any of his belongings. Presently the girl said, "Oh, it is leaking on me. This roof, it leaks." Her brother said, "Isn't that strange? There is no leak here by my bed." She kept on, kept on talking about the leak. He got tired of listening to her. He had made very long beds. "Well," he said, "you may come and lie at the foot of my bed." She did that. Still she was not satisfied. She was not close enough to him, you see. She began to complain again. "It leaks, it leaks!" He wondered, "Why? Why should it be leaking?" He did not believe it. After a while he got up. He went outdoors and looked. "There is no rain! Lots of stars, and clear!" And he thought, "What is wrong with her anyway?" He said to her, "Why, there is no rain. It is quite clear outside." Nevertheless she kept on crying out. After a while he told her, "Lie down at the back of my bed, next to the wall." She did that. Pretty soon she cried out again, "Oh, this is leaking over here." Then he knew, "Oh, she must want something." She cried out again and he told her, "Well, you may cover with my own cover." Now they were to sleep under the same blanket. She did that. She shut up then. She did not cry out. They went bad then. And right away she became pregnant.

After a while their baby was born. It was a boy. Every day the father would take his baby boy and they would go and sit on top of the roof of the house. He would sit there with that baby, so the baby would not cry. The mother heard somebody yelling on the other side of the river, daily. She looked across, "Oh, my! That is grandmother." Every day grandmother would call out, "Come across and get me." But they were afraid of her. No one knows what that grandmother might have done if they had gone across for her. It is possible that she would have made up with them. On the other hand she may have come just to kill them. Anyhow that brother just sat on the roof with his son, and the sister just stayed indoors out of sight. Wild Woman would call nicely, "Come and get me, dear grandchildren! I am [have been] searching for you. Come and get me!" He would not go across for her. Perhaps he should have gone in the house. Finally she knew they would never come for her. She had her walking cane with her. She said, "All right, you do not want to get me." She took her walking cane, she pointed it at the man on the roof. She said, "You drop dead!" He dropped dead. But the baby was not killed. The mother in the house would not show her face outside. She was afraid of Wild Woman. The baby cried and cried. The mother called out, "Bring the baby in the house." No answer. Wild Woman went away.

Finally the mother saw, "Grandmother is gone." She went outdoors then. Ah! Her husband was lying dead. She wept and wept. She took that baby and fastened him on her back. She left her husband lying; she set the house on fire. There was no neighbor near her, she was just by herself. Ah! It just broke her heart. She wanted to jump into that fire with her husband; but she did not like to take her baby with her into the fire.

Now there was a man who liked to go along the beach and watch to see what might be washed ashore. This very day he was going along the beach. This man was Bald Eagle. He looked, "Well! There is a house burning. I am going there. I wonder if the people are burned up, or what has happened?" He got there, he saw a woman with a baby on her back. "My goodness! That woman acts strangely; she acts as if she wants to jump into that fire. My goodness! I want to grab that baby if I can." He listened to that woman crying. She said, "Oh, my brother-husband! Upper half, brother! Lower half, husband!" He listened. He thought, "Oh! Does that not sound queer? One-half brother, one-half husband? I wonder who she is?" He did not get to talk to her at all. She became somewhat crazy. He got there just in time to seize that baby, and away! She jumped into the fire! He wanted to save her also, but he was unable to do it.

"Oh, I am not going down to the beach again. I am going to turn around and go right back home and bring this baby to my wife." Bald Eagle started home then. That baby cried and cried. He jiggled him, he still cried. He put him inside his shirt. Still he cried. He tried everything, but no, he could not make that baby become quiet. That little boy just cried and cried. "Oh goodness! Whatever can I do with him?" Bald Eagle worried. Bald Eagle and his wife had one child, a daughter. She was small yet, but she was a talker! She was a cranky little devil, that little girl. Bald Eagle kept thinking, "Oh, how am I going to keep that bad girl of ours from knowing I have gotten this baby?" At last he had an idea. He put that baby boy between his legs. Right up close to his testicles he placed the baby. Then that baby kept still; he stopped crying because no one could see him then; he was hidden.

Bald Eagle arrived at home. He called his wife aside and told her what had happened. He said, "I saved a little boy; I want you to [pretend to] become ill, and lie down as if you are going to have a baby." When night came, they told their little girl, "You must go to bed, early." She had a separate room. She went to bed. She did not like it a bit. After a while Bald Eagle took the baby out from between his legs and handed him to his wife. Pretty soon that baby squawked. The little girl had her covers open, she was peeping. She thought, "Huh! That is no new just-born baby. That is a big strong kind of baby." Next morning the mother acted as if she were ill. She remained in bed and Bald Eagle waited on her. But the little girl, she knew all the time!

The little boy grew very rapidly. In what seemed like no time at all, he could walk already. They told the little girl, "He is your little brother. You do not want to fight with him. Do not hit him."

After some time Bald Eagle went to that place where the house had been burned up. He went there and looked around. He found a rib of the man which had not been all burned up. He picked that up. He looked some more, he found the ankle bone of the baby's mother. He picked them up. He came home, he said, "These are for the baby. He can play ball with them. This round bone will be his ball, and he can strike it with this long bone." That little girl, she had a playhouse outdoors. Whenever the little boy hit his ball, the girl would run and get in the way of the ball so it would hit her. Then she would bawl. She would say, "Oh! He hit me! He is playing with his mother's ankle and his father's rib, and he hit me!" The little baby boy would hear that. It just broke his heart. He was getting bigger and of course he was getting smarter, because he was to become very smart indeed. He would run in the house. "Mother! Sister said I was playing with my mother's ankle bone, and I was playing with my father's rib bone." Oh, they went after that girl, they abused her dreadfully. They gave her a beating. As the boy grew bigger he began to abuse his sister also. He became so he himself would hit her purposely with that ball. She would put her hands up in front of her face like this [palms outward at the sides of her cheeks]. She would say, "Do not hit me! Do not hit me!" And she would cry and cry and wipe her nose. Her nose grew long and sharp from that continual wiping. Her eyes grew smaller and smaller from constant weeping. Her parents would abuse her just to treat the boy better. They thought the world of that baby boy. Finally the little girl's hands grew up at the sides of her face and she could not take them down any more. Her eyes almost disappeared, and her nose was even longer and sharper. She became Mole.

When the boy became a young man his [foster] parents sent him to the woods [to obtain a spirit power]. They said, "You go into the woods. Go and learn something." He did that. He became most powerful. He learned many things [acquired guardian spirits]. He obtained Thunder Bird as a guardian. That gave him power to fly around, just like Thunder Bird. He came home and told his father and mother; he did not know he was not supposed to tell anyone about his power. That Mole felt terribly jealous of him. They treated him better than her, though she was their own child. He told his people, "Well, mother! Father! I am going to leave you. I have learned many things [acquired many spirit powers]. I can even go and fly in the sky." They became very proud of him. They decided to tell him about himself. They told him, "Your mother jumped in the fire. Your father died. That Wild Woman, she is the one who killed your father. Your mother grieved so, just as soon as I grabbed you from your mother's back she jumped in the fire then." The boy's feelings were not hurt by this news; he thought this way, "I have a good father and mother in these people. They have treated me so well, I have never known any difference from having my own father and mother." They told him that Wild Woman was living in a certain town. He said, "I am going to kill her. I will take my sister along with me." Then he tried to teach his sister to fly, but she could not do it. She would fly just a short distance, and then she would drop down. She could not fly. He said to her, "Well, I would like to take you along; you could be my comrade and do some different sort of damage for me." She wanted to do that, but she could not fly, so they had to stop and study. Then her brother asked, "Can you go under the ground? Let's see you try." He sent her, she started out. She went under the ground, indeed she went swiftly. He could see the ground moving where she went along underneath, he saw that she went fast. He called, "Stop! Now you can come out." She came out. The father and mother were watching their children. Her brother said, "Do you think you can do that all the time?" Mole replied, "Yes, that does not trouble me at all." "All right! That is the way you will go!" Then he explained to Mole where they were going, and he told her, "If I am seen, those people will get excited and they will all come out to look at me while I fly around close to that town. You will go under the ground and come up inside the houses and take all those people's valuables, such as their money beads [large and valuable dentalia]."

So they started off. Mole had a soft rush basket with her in which to put whatever she might take. Oh, the old folks hated to see them both leaving; both of their children would be gone. The brother flew, he arrived at the town. Ice lived there. Ice was the first one to come outside. He looked up. Oh, he yelled, "Hey! Come out all you people. Everybody, come out! The strangest thing I ever saw, it is a bird with person's feet." Everyone ran outside to look. Presently Wild Woman came out. She was the same old woman but she was disguised as a young girl. She was wearing a basket cap.[1] He recognized her in that basket cap, nevertheless. Blue Jay had told him about her. Wild Woman was aware of all that. She came outside, she looked up. "Oh, that is Placed-Next-to-Testicles," she said. That made the young man angry, he did not like it that she named him that, and he did not like it that she knew him already. After a while he flew down and grabbed Wild Woman by the hair and away he took her. After a while her cap dropped down, but he paid no attention to that. He thought, "Everything is all right as long as I have her herself." He flew far, far out over the ocean; he tore her all to pieces and dropped the pieces in the water. He flew back home. He found his sister, she was back also, she arrived at the same time. She had many things which she had stolen. He said, "Maybe I killed her, Wild Woman. I seized her, I took her out over the ocean, I tore her to bits." His father and mother advised him, "You had better try looking every day. You had better go all over to different towns and places and see if you did kill her for good [forever]."

He said to Mole, his sister, "Well, we must go again." Mole emptied her basket. She gave all those things to her mother. Then they went. They arrived at a different place. Again Ice came out first. He called out again in the same manner for everyone to come out and look. Everyone came out. Lo! Wild Woman came out! She was alive! There she was in her basket cap. She said, "Oh, that is Placed-Next-to-Testicles." Then he flew down and grabbed her. As he flew off with her, her cap dropped down again. He did not know there was any meaning to that cap always dropping down. He took her out over the ocean, he tore her to pieces. He went home. He got there, his little sister arrived at the same time. She had gotten her soft rush basket half full of valuables. He said, "Maybe I killed her, Wild Woman. She was alive, I found her." His people advised him, "You cannot be sure. You see she is a different sort from a real person."

Next day he had to go again to see if Wild Woman had come back to life. The same thing that day, and the next day. The fifth day he went. His sister went underground again. As he flew along Blue Jay came. She said, "Nephew! You are on your way to kill Wild Woman?" "Yes, auntie." "Ah, she is fooling you all the time. If you really want to kill her, you must watch that basket cap. That is where her heart is, in that basket cap. You watch it. If you get it, you mash it up. Mash the crown up. That is her heart; her whole life lies there." "Yes, auntie. Is that all?" "That is all. You will surely get her if you do that." He went, Ice saw him. He yelled for everybody to come out. "A funny bird! He has person's feet!" Presently Wild Woman came out. She was alive. She had her cap on. She said,

---

1 Tillamook girls wore basket caps during their first mensis ceremonial and for one year following.

"Oh, that is Placed-Next-to-Testicles." He flew down, grabbed her, and he took that basket cap away from her so it could not drop down any more. (Wild Woman must have been surprised. That Blue Jay tells all the time. Whenever you are in trouble of any kind she will tell you what to do.) He took Wild Woman out over the ocean, he tore her to pieces, he threw her in the water. He took that basket cap, he tore it, he mashed it up, he threw it in the water. Now he came away, he got home. He told, "I met old auntie Blue Jay; she told me what to do. I did that. Maybe Wild Woman is dead now." His sister was home too. Next day, he said, "I had better go look for her again, to see if she has come back to life this time." His sister started also. He stopped at the first town. Ice saw him, he came out. Everyone came out. There was no Wild Woman in that town. He left, going on to the next town. Ice, he was there already! He saw the young man flying, called everybody to come out. Wild Woman was not there. In this manner he went on to those towns. He went on to the last town. Ice saw him again, everybody came out. She was not there either. She was dead. He had killed her. He came home. He said, "Maybe I killed her this time. She was not anywhere."

Then he talked to his father and mother. "Well, my people! I must leave you. I am going to leave this place. I cannot take my sister. I like her, but since she is unable to fly I cannot take her." Oh, those old people did not like it. His mother felt badly. She wept. He told her, "I cannot stay around here. I do not like it around here." He said, "Just the same, I think a great deal of you, my people." He left. Mole had to remain with the old folks.

He went, he flew away. He went up in the sky. He got there. "A strange place." He wandered about, he did not know where he was going because he had never been there before. After a while he came to a place. "Ah, I am going into that house." He found a huge old man. He was larger than any common person, he was very big indeed. The old man had a beautiful daughter but no wife. They invited him to stay there. They fed him. They liked him. The old man said, "You stay here. If you can do what I ask of you, you may have my daughter. She will be your wife." "All right." Then the old man told him, "I have some trees burning. You go and look at those trees." Those trees were standing erect, they kept burning all the time. They were full of pitch. Many young men had tried to win that daughter, and they had all been killed. The daughter, ah! she liked this young man. She wished in her heart, "I do hope he does not get killed." She liked him. He went, he saw those trees burning. That hot pitch, if it should drop on a person, that was how a person would be killed. He would be burned to death. He looked, "I am not going to go near them. That is how the old man thought I would get killed. He had a trap for me, but I am not going to be killed." He looked at those trees. He decided, "Ice will appear around all those trees. It will put that fire out." That happened. Ice formed all around those trees and put that fire out. It made a terrifying noise, like thunder. The girl heard the noise, "Ah, that old father of mine.[2] I fear that young man is killed now." She felt badly. Presently he came back. He said, "Dad, you have no trees burning, those fires are gone out." "Well," replied the old man, "they never go out. They are burning steadily all the time." The old man, he started out to look at them. He got there, all those trees were out. They were coal black. He thought, "That is strange. Is he going to beat me?" He went home.

He said to the young man, "I want you to go and look at my dogs." He called them his dogs, but they were really grizzlies. He had informed those grizzlies, "If that fellow comes, you bears tear him to pieces and eat him up." The young man asked the girl, "What does your father do with those dogs?" She told him, "Oh, they are animals. They are grizzly bears, they kill people." The young man went. He saw those two grizzly bears. He went up close to them. He took them by the neck, one in each hand, he slammed them on the ground, he killed them. It caused a loud noise, like thunder. They were dead, both of them. The girl heard the noise. She thought, "I guess the young man has been killed all right." She felt badly. Presently he came back. He said, "Dad, you have no dogs. They are dead." The old fellow went to see for himself. They were surely dead. Blood was running from their mouths. "That does look as if he will indeed get the better of me," the old man thought. He went back.

He told the young man, "I dropped my sledge hammer in the lake. Will you go down, dive for it?" "Are you quite sure you dropped it overboard?" "Yes, I did." That was another trap for him. He went, he dived down. He thought, "Well, if he did not drop it over, I shall find one anyway. I will show him that I would not come up without one. I will certainly bring one." The old man stood right there. As soon as he had dived, the old man spoke, "Now all over that lake there will be solid ice. Thus he cannot come up again." He was going to kill that young fellow. He-who-had-dived tried to come up. His head bounced back from solid ice. He had a sledge hammer in his hand. He had magically caused one to be on the bottom of the lake. He took his sledge hammer, he broke that ice, he came up. He had brought back the hammer. He said, "Here is your rock [hammer]."

Now there was but one remaining trap [trial]. The old man said, "I have a [fish] trap. I catch fish in this trap. You go see if there are any fish. Bring me some fish." He went. No fish! There was the trap, but no fish. He made himself into a small fish. He thought, "I shall be a small one. He is a big man and he will be disgusted. He will not want to eat a small fish." He turned himself into a little, tiny steel head. He wished, "I want him to bandage my eyes when he cooks me, so they will not be burned. And he shall not eat me. I shall contain quantities of oil. He will catch my oil in the trough, and he will keep drinking that oil. It will make him sleepy, he will lie down and forget me. He is not going to eat

2 He is Thunder.

me." The old man heard a loud noise, like thunder. He laughed, "Aha! My son-in-law, he makes so much noise." He went to the fish trap. "Oh, my goodness! Such a little fish!" He was disgusted. He did not cook it right away. He almost forgot it. He left it in his soft rush basket out by the door. After a while he said, "Oh, I almost forgot that little fish." It was nearly evening. He went out and got it. He was going to cook it by the fire. He did bandage the eyes of that little fish. Soon he saw a lot of oil dripping down. He took his trough and set it there. In almost no time at all it was full. He kept drinking that oil. He got satisfied. "I am not going to eat that fish. I am too full." After a while he set the sticks with the fish in the corner. "Some other time I will eat it. Maybe in the morning." His daughter would have liked to have killed him. The old man went to bed. It was night. Everyone went to bed. Very soon that old man was asleep.

The young fellow climbed off the stick, he went to the river and bathed in the dark. He came back in the house, he went to his wife, to that girl. He crawled in bed with her. Oh! She gave him a beating. She thought this way, "He is dead already. He is cooked. This must be some other man coming to my bed." He said to her, "Why do you beat me? I thought you felt badly about me. I came back. Your father could not kill me." She felt happy then. The next morning the old man got up. He fixed his fire. "I guess I will go and eat my little fish now." He found only the stick there, there was no fish. He puzzled, "I wonder how that fish went away? A cooked fish!" Then his daughter got up, and his son-in-law got up. Now all those trials were past, he had beaten the old man in all those things. Now he would live there.

His-Bones-Have-Been-Sucked lived next door. His-Bones-Have-Been-Sucked used to have a strong power. He had tried to win Thunder Bird's daughter. He had almost beaten the old man except for the last trial. When he went to the fish trap he had made himself into too large a fish, and old man Thunder Bird had eaten him and sucked all his bones. When His-Bones-Have-Been-Sucked made himself over he was not much good any more. He was weak, he had lost his voice. He was not permitted to marry the old man's daughter, but he was a neighbor. Thunder's son-in-law made friends with His-Bones-Have-Been-Sucked. He felt sorry for him. All of the men in that place went out in big canoes to spear whales, far out in the ocean. His-Bones-Have-Been-Sucked would go alone. He could catch only scrub whales because he was no longer strong. Thunder's son-in-law asked His-Bones-Have-Been-Sucked, "Do you go to catch whale?" "Yes, I go." "May I go along with you?" "Oh, surely," said His-Bones-Have-Been-Sucked, "you can go with me." Then he told him his plan. He said to His-Bones-Have-Been-Sucked, "I will braid my hair in two braids, I will look like a woman. I will steer your canoe. You will be on the bow, you will do all the spearing. You talk back. Talk big! When those fellows call to you, you say, 'Come on! Let us make lightning so we can see the whale!'" Indeed they went out in the canoe in that manner. The other men said to each other, "What is wrong with His-Bones-Have-Been-Sucked? He never acted that way before. He always acted downhearted all the time." Then they wondered, "Who is that woman he has? Maybe it is Thunder's daughter. But she never went with him before." Thunder's son-in-law asked His-Bones-Have-Been-Sucked, "When you were young, when you were strong, what kind of whales did you used to catch?" "Oh," said His-Bones-Have-Been-Sucked, "I caught the very best then." Thunder's son-in-law told him, "Well, you can have your pick of them today. You spear, I will help you with my power." The other men could not make good lightning. They saw that His-Bones-Have-Been-Sucked made lightning like daylight! They said, "Goodness! His-Bones-Have-Been-Sucked has changed. He is getting different." They talked about it for some time. After a while one said, "Do you suppose Placed-Next-to-Testicles came up here?" They understood it then. His-Bones-Have-Been-Sucked got a very large and special kind of whale that day. The very best kind. But the other men finally found out that it was Placed-Next-to-Testicles who went with His-Bones-Have-Been-Sucked, the weak.

Old man Thunder loved the tail part of a whale. He would cut it off and run a stake through it and put it by the fire with his big trough under it for the oil to drip in. The old man's roasting stick was one half of a big fir tree. Tonight Thunder's son-in-law wished, "I hope that big stick will burn and break off." Very soon it burned, it broke. The old man said, "Well! That never happened like that before. I have had that same stick for all time. I wonder how that happened?" After a while he decided, "I will just have to get a fir tree and split it in two. I need a stake." He went, he took his wedge and his hammer, he got a big tree, he was going to split it in two. His son-in-law looked on, he watched him. He wished, "I hope that wedge will drop into a crack in that tree and he will reach for it. I hope the wedge will fly out and his hand will get pinched hard, and hurt badly." That was just what happened. The old man's daughter knew her husband had done that. She told him, "How you abuse the old man!" He got hurt very severely, that wedge flew too far away, he could not reach it. He simply could not. He suffered dreadfully. Thunder and lightning [roared and flashed]. When that old man was suffering he looked around. That [his glance] made lightning. Finally old man Thunder called Raven. He said, "Come and help me out. Move that wedge closer to me." Raven was not strong. That wedge was so large he could not lift it. Raven tried so hard to lift it that the skin between his toes split. Finally he got it moved enough so the old man could reach it with his foot. Then with his foot he dragged that wedge in, picked it up, and split that tree with one blow. His hand was all swelled. He paid Raven many pieces of whale meat. Raven was very glad.

All gone.

SIOUX[1]

Many Indian stories focus on complex interpersonal dynamics of common relationships. These stories often begin with a situation of socio-psychological instability: here a family unit of one man with two wives, his brother with none. The imbalance opens the initiating actions to a variety of interpretations. The story does not aim at a singular meaning, but instead generates a diversity of possible meanings. This encourages retelling, which is the "same" narrative only in regard to some elements of content – features of social situation, event, character, etc. This is why a modern reader needs to remember that normally a story was familiar to Indian listeners. They heard a narrative with an awareness (unavailable to us) of its history, of different meanings developed from it by previous tellers. That awareness was fostered by a narrative structure built upon schematic patterns of parallelism and contrast, an artifice not controlled by natural time sequences.

Hazardous conditions of physical survival made Sioux listeners aware that even small issues of interpersonal relations might be of life or death significance in a small community. To them, the account of the brother's refusal of his sister-in-law's request for the owl would have suggested multiple explanations. There are the obvious alternatives of interpreting the request either as a command or a sexual invitation, but beyond these are other questions, for example, might the hunter's refusal originate in selfishness or jealousy? Deciding among such alternatives requires the listener to evaluate how this first episode will relate to subsequent ones, regardless of their sequential order. For Indian listeners who knew the story, "suspense" consisted primarily in how a teller,

---

1 Sioux is now the commonest general name for peoples often identified by other tribal names such as Lakota or Dakota.

through manipulations of parallelism and contrast between various events, would create a particular moral–psychological meaningfulness to the narrative. The reduction of the importance of temporal sequence and escape from direct cause–effect relations free an auditor's imagination to engage in an exploration of new perspectives and diverse and complex possibilities of the meaning of the story's actions. We who read silently to ourselves must remember an Indian heard the story in company with others. She heard it retold by someone with whom she had listened to it before. Later, she would hear other retellings; perhaps retell it herself. For her, the story was not a detached, fixed text, but a set of specific social experiences involving a variety of people exchanging ideas, opinions, convictions, and experiences. "The" story for her is a long-term series of social negotiations, which over time refine and subtilize its form and complicate its significance so that, despite its brevity, it is packed with meanings inseparable from actual interpersonal relationships.

We can't recover the processes of this communal activity of storytelling, but we can recognize that it bears some resemblance to our pleasure in stories we value the most, what we call classics, which are narratives that we enjoy rereading. That may encourage us to seek reward in grappling imaginatively with problems posed by such an Indian story as this, finding for ourselves possible ethical and psychological connections between episodes apparently unrelated by progress of the plot. For instance, we may find it worth assessing the significance of the story's final event, in which the tribal group is destroyed through an over-killing of buffalo by the man who refused his sister-in-law a single owl.

Another difficulty for us, however, is that most of the actions are grotesquely exaggerated and fantastically violent – especially in representing women as threats to men. It may help in understanding this characteristic narrative extremism to recognize its connection with the formulaic "If he had not done so-and-so," conditions would be different from what they are now. The tale evokes imagining of actions and impulses which accepted cultural practice suppresses or condemns. The storytelling frees listeners to imagine communally emotions and impulses subjected to the strongest social controls. This story, for example, magnifies to sensational imaginative visibility Sioux men's unspoken fears of women's sexual potencies. Unrealistic exaggeration allows depiction of common psychic attitudes that one doesn't offer openly for either private or communal evaluation. What seems at first glance to be extreme, excessive, and bizarre represents the terrific and terrifying power of our hidden emotions and the strain we feel in accommodating them to our social ideals. Sioux men were brave hunters – consider carefully if you would have what it takes to kill a buffalo with a bow and arrow (so you control your horse only with your knees) as you ride bareback in the middle of a stampeding herd of two hundred huge animals. Sioux were also extraordinarily courageous warriors: they paid highest tribute to those who "counted coup" – in the midst of a battle, touched an enemy without killing or wounding him (which, of course, puts your own life at the highest risk). Most of them also were loyal husbands and *responsible members of the tribe. These impressive qualities were achieved by self-application of cultural ideals to the instincts, anxieties, and fears that all human beings experience. It is not difficult to guess the kind of relief such men might feel in hearing a story that articulates feelings they have had so persistently to control. It seems likely that, in different ways for all Sioux listeners, the extreme fantasies of this story were sustaining to them both as individuals and as members of their community. To Sioux women, who both told and listened to such stories, the bringing into imaginative openness of the psychic pressures felt by their men must surely have been helpful. We must not forget that these people, in the harsh and unforgiving conditions of the high plains, had built a special way of life of which they were intensely proud. And justifiably proud, for it has been admired by virtually every Westerner not bent on genocide who has encountered it, in actuality or in historical reports. It was a culture founded upon and continually renewed by this kind of "exaggerated" storytelling that is perhaps the only way of telling both the private and public truth about any people's profoundest feelings and ideals.*

5
From Clark Wissler, "Some Dakota Myths II," *Journal of American Folklore* 20 (1907), 195–206, 197–9.

A man lived with his two wives and a brother. One day the brother went out to hunt, and as he was coming back he shot an owl, which he brought home with him. As he was coming up toward the brother's tipi, his sister-in-law met him and asked for the owl. The brother refused to give it to her. Then she cried. She took a sharp stone, scratched her face and thighs, and went to her husband in that condition. She said that her brother-in-law had inflicted these wounds trying to lie with her. This made the husband very angry. So he sent for a friend, and directed him to take his brother out to an island and leave him there. The friend did this, and when he returned received the woman who caused the trouble for his wife.

The brother lived alone on the island. He could find nothing to eat but rose berries. He soon ate all of these, but was still hungry. One day, while he was sleeping, he heard a noise near him, and, looking down, saw three wild turnips pushing up from the ground. He took these and they supplied him with food for several days. But at last they were eaten, and he became very hungry again. One day, while he was sleeping, he heard a noise, and, looking around, saw a small animal. He caught this animal, took out his paint bag, and painted him, praying to him for some kind of power to get to the mainland. Then he released the animal. It at once plunged into the lake, disappeared under the water, and presently there arose in its place a very large animal with big horns. The monster spoke to the brother, directed him to climb on his back and take hold of his horns. "Now," said the monster, "I shall take you to the shore, but you must watch the sky, and if you see a cloud you must tell me." So they started, the man holding the monster's horns. When they were near the shore, the brother saw a cloud. Now the brother was afraid that if he told the monster about the cloud, the monster would dive into the water and he would be drowned. So he kept quiet and said nothing about the cloud. Just as they reached the shore, and the brother sprang off on dry land, the thunder came down from the cloud and killed the monster.

As the brother walked on he heard some women cry. They said, "Our grandfather is killed! Our grandfather is killed!" Looking around, the brother finally made out that the noise came from a buffalo skull lying on the ground. Looking inside, he saw a great many mice. "What are you doing in there?" he asked. Then he took them out and killed all of them.

Then the brother went on his way and presently came to a lodge where an old woman lived. As soon as the old woman saw him she cried out, "Oh, my son, my lost son!" She called the young man inside and cooked some meat for him. Now the brother was very sleepy, but was suspicious of the woman, so he lay quietly and watched. After a while the woman took some paint and began to rub it on one of her legs. As she did so, the leg became exceedingly large. This was the way the old woman killed people. While she was doing this, the brother sprang up and stabbed her with a crane's bill which he always carried with him. The old woman screamed, and the brother sprang out of the lodge as quickly as possible. Presently he came back, and, peering in, he saw the body of the old woman lying in the fire. Then he gathered together much wood and threw it into the fire. In this way he burned up not only the body of the old woman, but the entire lodge. If he had not done this, women would still have the power to increase the size and strength of their legs to such a degree that they could kill men with them.

He went on his journey and came to another lodge. Looking in, he saw a woman. When she saw him, she invited him to come in, and began to cook some meat for him. As he sat watching her, he saw that she had a hole in the top of her head. As she cooked she took out some of her brains and mixed them with the meat in the pot. Now the brother called up his friend the gopher. This was the animal that had helped him to get away from the island. The brother directed the gopher to watch the woman at her cooking, and if the food was dangerous to gnaw a hole in the bottom of the pot, so that the soup might run down into the ground. Then the brother lay down as if to sleep. The gopher gnawed a hole in the bottom of the pot so that the food all ran from the pot into his hole in the ground. Then the brother pretended to eat from the pot. Then he lay down on his bed as if in deep sleep. This is the way this woman killed people. She mixed poisonous soup for them, and after they had eaten they became unconscious and died. Now the brother watched the woman, and when she lay down to sleep he arose, and taking a hot stone from the fire dropped it into the holes in her head. The woman sprang up, the hot stone sputtered and sizzled. The woman reeled, screamed, and fell down dead. Then the brother threw the body into the fire and burned it up, together with all her belongings. If he had not done this, women would still mix the poison of their brains with the food they cook.

As the brother went on again he came to another lodge. An old woman was looking out, and he heard her say, "There comes a man." A voice from inside said, " I have seen such a thing before." The old woman invited him to enter. Fine food was set before him. There were two beautiful girls there. Each had a bed on opposite sides of the lodge. When night came each invited the brother to bed. As he did not move, the girls fell to disputing as to which he would choose. At last the brother settled the argument by going to one of the beds. Now these girls had teeth in the vagina, and when they were aroused the teeth could be heard grating upon each other. The brother heard the noise. He took his crane's bill, thrust it into the vagina and upward, killing the girl. Then he went over to the other bed and did the same. Then he went on his way. If he had not done this to these girls, all women would be dangerous to their lovers.

Then he continued his journey, and presently saw a cloud on the top of a hill. As he went on, he turned around and saw many animals following him. They were of all kinds, and he was afraid. Then he saw there was a woman with them. He threw away his clothes, painted his body with mud, and, taking a cane, walked bent over like an old person. Then the woman called all the animals back, saying, "You must not hurt such an old man." Then the woman spoke to the brother and told him that he would find some old weak animals in the rear that would serve him as food. When the man went to look for them, he found nothing but skunks, porcupines, and badgers. He killed some of them, however, and ate them. This is how people came to eat the flesh of animals.

As he went on he came to another lodge. He saw a poor woman going out for water. When he came up to her, he saw that she was his sister. She told him that her husband was very cruel to her and always beat her when he came home. Now the brother told her to go in to her husband as before and say nothing. The brother stood outside. When the man began to beat the woman he sprang into the lodge and struck down the cruel husband. Because he did this it has come to pass that cruel husbands are punished by their wife's relatives.

As he continued on his way, he came to the camp of his people. His brothers lived here and also his father, who was now very old. They were all glad to see their long-lost brother, and the father was so glad that he died from the excitement. One day the young man went out to hunt and killed a great many buffalo. He killed so many that when the meat was piled up it looked like a hill. Then he returned to the camp and told his people to take their horses and go out for the meat. When they came to the place they found that birds and animals in great numbers had come from every direction to eat the meat. When the people came up the animals fell upon them, and all the people were destroyed. That is why animals now eat the flesh of men.

ORIGINS

In the Sioux story about the younger brother we encountered such phrases as "If he had not done this, all women would be dangerous to their lovers." Statements like this appear again and again in Native American stories, many of which begin, "This is why..." or conclude, "that is how," for example, "the beaver came to have a broad tail." These seeming explanations of origin are usually not to be taken at face value. Sometimes they are ironic jokes, and they are often rhetorical devices, formal announcements that a story is about to be told, or that it has now ended. And even stories genuinely concerned with the origin of some creature or custom or character-istic of man or the natural world normally were not told or listened to as literally factual accounts. The "explanatory" phrases are signals of imaginative narratives about what no one can with absolute certainty know the complete truth. Their function is to arouse the audience's imagination to attend carefully to some facts of nature, some ethical issues, or some historical traditions. Such stories in an oral culture may serve something of the function of an encyclopedia, as does the Cherokee story (6).

Major "origin" myths that are foundational for a tribe's religion and mytho-logical system are, of course, to be taken seriously (although frequently they include amusing features). But their seriousness would be undermined if they were treated as only literally realistic. Their high significance arises from their proven efficacy in concentrating thought and feeling on primary cultural principles by dramatizing their profound congruence with basic processes of the natural world. Thus the Gros Ventre myth (7), which belongs to the type ethnologists classify as "Earth Diver" (see also the Seneca myth (9) of the woman who falls from the sky), compels its audience to imagine elemental features of the environment as dynamically emerging out of one another. The primary animating power of the cosmos is identified with the movement of invisible air, the breath of earthly life. Air shaped into shout, word, and song permits purposeful human consciousness to enter as a specially creative force into the perpetual interchanges that are the physical world.

Re-creation is an ideal theme for oral storytelling, because each telling re-performs earlier recitations in a new way, thereby opening possibilities for innovative interpretation. This is why all mythographers now accept Claude Lévi-Strauss's principle that each myth is in fact constituted not by a core narrative, not by some essential meaning, but by the sum of all its retellings. Myths, like species of organisms, persist by evolving. Those that offer an account of how a particular cultural practice came into being enable teller and listeners to re-examine what Pierre Bourdieu has called the habitus, the most traditional, customary, unthinkingly accepted ways of doing things of any social group. Myths that affirm the importance of a specific ritual, or condemn some tabooed behavior, or assert the cosmic origin of some institution, simultaneously expose the ritual, behavior, or institution to self-conscious evaluation. Such a myth telling of an imagined origin necessarily reveals in the clear light of present actualities of tribal life its subject's raison d'être. In Native American myths revered traditions always thus appear in terms of their relevance to present historical circumstances. This is why the retelling of sacred myths is for Indians inspirational, not the mere formal rehearsal of what is respected only because it is ancient. The central Indian myths are not simply coercive, nor rote reiterations of dogma. They enable the habitus to remain vital, capable of adapting itself to both environmental changes (for example, shifts in climate or the disappearance of traditional food sources) and to societal transformations, such as those produced by war or effects of epidemic disease, or contact with other peoples with different cultural practices. Indians telling of crucial origins simultaneously re-empower both the sacred potency of the natural world and a particular form of civilization.

CHEROKEE (A)

This Cherokee story about the animals trying to capture fire identifies markings and behavioral characteristics of diverse creatures, concluding with a defining distinction between two related species of water spiders. Such stories are characteristically light-hearted, but also typically convey some moral insight: it would be foolish to scorn the little female insect who accomplishes what flashy male birds and large animals could not.

6
From James Mooney, *Myths of the Cherokees*. Washington, DC: Annual Report of the Bureau of American Ethnology 19 (1897–8) 3-575, 240.

In the beginning there was no fire, and the world was cold, until the Thunders sent their lightning and put fire into the bottom of a hollow sycamore tree which grew on an island. The animals knew it was there, because they could see the smoke coming out at the top, but they could not get to it on account of the water, so they had a council to decide what to do.

Every animal that could fly or swim was anxious to go after the fire. The Raven offered, and because he was so large and strong they thought he could surely do the job, so he was sent first. He flew high and far across the water and alighted on the sycamore tree, but while he was wondering what to do next, the heat had scorched all his feathers black, and he was frightened and came back without the fire. The little Screech Owl volunteered to go, and reached the place safely, but while he was looking down into the hollow tree a blast of hot air came up and nearly burned out his eyes. He managed to fly home, but it was a long time before he could see well, and his eyes are red to this day. Then the Hooting Owl and the Horned Owl went, but by the time they got to the hollow tree the fire was burning so fiercely that the smoke nearly blinded them, and the ashes carried up by the wind made white rings around their eyes. They had to come home again without the fire, but with all their rubbing they were never able to get rid of the white rings.

Now no more of the birds would venture, and so the little black Racer Snake said he would go through the water and bring back some fire. He swam across to the island and slithered through the grass to the tree, and went in by a small hole at the bottom. The heat and smoke were too much for him, too, and after dodging about blindly over the hot ashes until he was almost on fire himself he managed by good luck to get out again at the same hole. But his body had been scorched black, and he has ever since had the habit of darting and doubling back on his track as if trying to escape from uncomfortable confinement. He came back, and the great Blacksnake, "The Climber" offered to go for fire. He swam over to the island and climbed up the tree on the outside, as the great Blacksnake always does, but when he put his head down into the hole the smoke choked him so that he fell into the burning stump, and before he could climb out he was as black as the little Racer.

Now they held another council, for still there was no fire, and the world was cold, but birds, snakes, and four-footed animals all had some excuse for not going, because they were all afraid to venture near the burning sycamore, until at last the Water Spider said she would go. This is not the water spider that looks like a mosquito, but the other one, with black downy hair and red stripes on her body. She can run on top of the water or dive to the bottom, so there would be no trouble to get over to the island, but the question was, how could she bring back the fire? "I'll manage that," said the Water Spider; so she spun a thread from her body and wove it into a *tusti* bowl, which she fastened on her back. Then she crossed over to the island and through the grass to where the fire was still burning. She put one little coal of fire into her bowl, and came back with it, and ever since we have had fire, and the Water Spider still keeps her *tusti* bowl.

GROS VENTRE

The Gros Ventre myth (which like all such myths is told in order to be retold) in characteristic Indian fashion narrates a re-originating. In contrast to the Western fondness for a single, absolute beginning, as in the Old Testament and modern physicists' hypothesis of the Big Bang, Native Americans conceived of the cosmos as continuously self-recreative. They understood their oral cultures persisted only by continually self-renewing, retelling old stories in new ways. And they believed that thus to renew one's civilization was to make a distinctively human contribution to the continuous processes of revitalization constituting the cosmos.

7

From A. L. Kroeber, *Ethnology of the Gros Ventre*. New York: Anthropological Papers of the American Museum of Natural History 1, Part 4 (1907), 141–281, 60–1.

The people before the present people were wild. They did not know how to do anything. Nixant did not like the way they lived and acted. He thought, "I will make a new world." He had the chief pipe. He went outside and hung the pipe on three sticks. He picked up four buffalo-chips. One he put under each of the sticks on which the pipe hung, and one he took for his own seat. He said, "I will sing three time and shout three times. After I have done these things, I will kick the earth and water will come out of the crack. There will be heavy rain. There will be water all over the earth." Then he began to sing. After he had sung three times, he shouted three times. Then he kicked the ground and it cracked. The water came out, and it rained for days, and over all the earth was water.

By means of the buffalo-chips he and the pipe floated. Then it stopped raining. There was water everywhere. He floated wherever the wind took him. For days he drifted that way. Above him the Crow flew about. All the other birds and animals were drowned. The Crow became tired. It flew about crying, " My father, I am becoming tired. I want to rest." Three times it said this. After it had said so three times, Nixant said, "Alight on the pipe and rest." Repeatedly the Crow cried to him, and each time was allowed to alight on the pipe. Nixant became tired sitting in one position. He cried. He did not know what to do. After he had cried a long time, he began to unwrap the chief pipe. The pipe contained all animals. He selected those with long breath to dive through the water. First he selected the Large Loon. The Loon was not alive, but Nixant had its body wrapped up in the pipe. Nixant sang, and then commanded it to dive and try to bring mud. The Loon dived. It was not halfway down when it lost its breath and turned back. It came up almost drowned at the place where Nixant was. Then Nixant took the Small Loon's body and sang. Then Small Loon dived. It nearly reached the mud at the bottom. But then it lost its breath and went up again, and, nearly dead, reached the place where Nixant was. Then he took the Turtle. He sang and it became alive, and he sent it off and it dived. Meanwhile the Crow did not alight, but flew about crying for rest. Nixant did not listen to it. After a long time the turtle came up. It was nearly dead. It had filled its feet and the cracks along its sides with mud. When it reached Nixant all the mud had washed away and it was nearly dead. Nixant said, "Did you succeed in reaching the mud?" The turtle said, "Yes, I reached it. I had much of it in my feet and about my sides, but it all washed away from me before I came to you." Then Nixant said to it, "Come to me," and the Turtle went to him. Nixant looked at the inside of his feet and in the cracks of its sides. On the inside of its feet he found a little earth. He scraped this into his hand, began to sing. After he had sung three times, he shouted three times. Then he said, "I will throw this little dust that I have in my hand into the water. Little by little let there be enough to make a strip of land large enough for me." The he began to drop it, little by little, into the water, opening and closing his hand carefully. And when he had dropped it all, there was a little land, large enough for him to sit on. Then he said to the Crow, "Come down and rest. I have made a little piece of land for myself and you." Then the Crow came down and rested. After it had rested, it flew up again.

Then Nixant took out from his pipe two long wing feathers. He had one in each hand as he began to sing. After he had sung three times, he shouted three times, "youh, hon, hon," and spread his arms, and closed his eyes. When he had done this he said to himself, "Let there be land as far as my eyes can see around me." When he opened his eyes, there indeed was land all around. After he had made the land there was no water anywhere. He went about with his pipe and with the Crow. They were all there was to be seen in the world. Now Nixant became thirsty. He did not know what to do to get water. Then he thought, "I will cry." He cried. While he cried he closed his eyes. He tried to think how he could get water. He shed tears. His tears dropped to the ground. They made a large spring in front of him. Then a stream ran from the spring. When he stopped crying, a large river was flowing. Thus he made rivers and streams. . . .

CHEROKEE (B)

Adam and Eve's loss of paradise because of their deliberate disobedience is entirely lamentable. But the "fall" precipitated by the adolescents in this Cherokee myth liberates the boys from a condition of dependence on natural bounty – frees them to become mature, at the cost of arduous labor to obtain food either by hunting or farming. Their reward is developing into self-sufficient adults fully responsible for the character and quality of their way of life. The contrast of Cherokee and biblical narratives illustrates an essential difference between Native American and Judeo-Christian mythologizing: we distinguish absolutely between natural and supernatural – Indians literally fuse them.

Successful Hunter (Kana'tĭ) and Corn (Selu) are neither divinities nor ancestral Cherokee. They are humanized manifestations of the principal foods of the Indians. The Cherokee understood that they lived by destroying other lives, either plant or animal. Their society prospered through its civilized skills at hunting and farming. This narrative identifies biological maturation in the boys with developing cultural processes by which the Cherokee obtained their food. Their success at evolving culture out of nature explains why finally Kana'tĭ and Selu can receive with pleasure the boys who drove him away and killed her.

While their actions exemplify adolescent behavior, at least one is unusual. Wild Boy comes into being from the blood Selu has washed off killed game; he embodies the powers of blood and water, for later he becomes one of the far-traveling thunders who bring rain needed by corn. Although he appears long after Selu's son is born, Wild boy is treated as the elder. He leads the boys' "revolt." Perhaps he manifests the deepest stratum of a "normal" adolescent's psyche. The boys' curiosity leads them to discover the infinite fecundity of animals, a discovery which compels them to develop hunting skills. Next they "kill" Selu, corn that grew naturally. We nourish ourselves by crunching all those corn embryos between our teeth, but if we are to be sure of enough we must cultivate the plant. The boys learn, not as perfectly as they might, for they are human, to plant and care for seeds they transform into crops: nature is cultivated. They then **teach** *their skills to others: cultural tradition begins, ultimately fulfilled with the boys becoming mythic thunders. By telling a story of people undergoing simultaneously the crises of biological maturation and cultural transformation the myth dramatizes with amazing economy humanity's unique dependence upon learned control of the processes constituting our natural environment.*

8

From James Mooney, *Myths of the Cherokees*. Washington, DC: Annual Report of the Bureau of American Ethnology 19 (1897–8), 3–575; "Kana'tĭ and Selu," 242–8]

When I was a boy this is what the old men told me they had heard when they were boys.

Long years ago, soon after the world was made, a hunter and his wife lived at Pilot knob with their only child, a little boy. The father's name was Kana'tĭ (The Lucky Hunter), and his wife was called Selu (Corn). No matter when Kana'tĭ went into the wood, he never failed to bring back a load of game, which his wife would cut up and prepare, washing off the blood from the meat in the river near the house. The little boy used to play down by the river every day, and one morning the old people thought they heard laughing and talking in the bushes as though there were two children there. When the boy came home at night his parents asked him who had been playing with him all day. "He comes out of the water," said the boy, "and he calls himself my elder brother. He says his mother was cruel to him and threw him into the river." Then they knew that the strange boy had sprung from the blood of the game which Selu had washed off at the river's edge.

Every day when the little boy went out to play the other would join him, but as he always went back again into the water the old people never had a chance to see him. At last one evening Kana'tĭ said to his son, "Tomorrow, when the other boy comes to play, get him to wrestle with you, and when you have your arms around him hold on to him and call for us." The boy promised to do as he was told, so the next day as soon as his playmate appeared he challenged him to a wrestling match. The other agreed at once, but as soon as they had their arms around each other, Kana′tĭ's boy began to scream for his father. The old folks at once came running down, and as soon as the Wild Boy saw them he struggled to free himself and cried out, "Let me go; you threw me away!" but his brother held on until the parents reached the spot, when they seized the Wild Boy and took him home with them. They kept him in the house until they had tamed him, but he was always wild and artful in his disposition, and was the leader of his brother in every mischief. It was not long until the old people discovered that he had magic-powers, and they called him I′năge-utăsûñ′hĭ (He-who-grew-up-wild).

Whenever Kana′tĭ went into the mountains he always brought back a fat buck or doe, or maybe a couple of turkeys. One day the Wild Boy said to his brother, "I wonder where our father gets all that game; let's follow him next time and find out." A few days afterward Kana′tĭ took a bow and some feathers in his hand and started off toward the west. The boys waited a little while and then went after him, keeping out of sight until they saw him go into a swamp where there were a great many of the small reeds that hunters use to make arrowshafts. Then the Wild Boy changed himself into a puff of bird's down, which the wind took up and carried until it alighted upon Kana′tĭ's shoulder just as he entered the swamp, but Kana′tĭ knew nothing about it. The old man cut reeds, fitted the feathers to them and made some arrows, and the Wild Boy – in his other shape – thought, "I wonder what those things are for?" When Kana′tĭ had his arrows finished he came out of the swamp and went on again. The wind blew the down from his shoulder, and it fell in the woods, when the Wild Boy took his right shape again and went back and told his brother what he had seen. Keeping out of sight of their father, they followed him up the mountain until he stopped at a certain place and lifted a large rock. At once there ran out a buck, which Kana′tĭ shot, and then lifting it upon his back he started for home again. "Oho!" exclaimed the boys, "he keeps all the deer shut up in that hole, and whenever he wants meat he just lets one out and kills it with those things he made in the swamp." They hurried and reached home before their father, who had the heavy deer to carry, and he never knew that they had followed.

A few days later the boys went back to the swamp, cut some reeds, and made seven arrows, and then started up the mountain to where their father kept the game. When they got to the place, they raised the rock and a deer came running out. Just as they drew back to shoot it, another came out, and then another and another, until the boys got confused and forgot what they were about. In those days all the deer had their tails hanging down like other animals, but as a buck was running past the Wild Boy struck its tail with his arrow so that it pointed upward. The boys thought this good sport, and when the next one ran past the Wild Boy struck its tail so that it stood straight up, and his brother struck the next one so hard with his arrow that the deer's tail was almost curled over his back. The deer carries his tail this way ever since. The deer came running past until the last one had come out of the hole and escaped into the forest. Then came droves of raccoons, rabbits, and all the other four-footed animals – all but the bear, because there was no bear then. Last came great flocks of turkeys, pigeons, and partridges that darkened the air like a cloud and made such a noise with their wings that Kana'tï, sitting at home, heard the sound like distant thunder on the mountains and said to himself, "My bad boys have got into trouble; I must go and see what they are doing."

So he went up the mountain, and when he came to the place where he kept the game he found the two boys standing by the rock, and all the birds and animals were gone. Kana'tï was furious, but without saying a word he went down into the cave and kicked the covers off four jars in one corner, when out swarmed bedbugs, fleas, lice, and gnats, and got all over the boys. They screamed with pain and fright and tried to beat off the insects, but the thousands of vermin crawled over them and bit and stung them until both dropped down nearly dead. Kana'tï stood looking on until he thought they had been punished enough, when he knocked off the vermin and made the boys a talk. "Now, you rascals," said he, "you have always had plenty to eat and never had to work for it. Whenever you were hungry all I had to do was to come up here and get a deer or a turkey and bring it home for your mother to cook; but now you have let out all the animals, and after this when you want a deer to eat you will have to hunt all over the woods for it, and then maybe not find one. Go home now to your mother, while I see if I can find something to eat for supper."

When the boys got home again they were very tired and hungry and asked their mother for something to eat. "There is no meat," said Selu, "but wait a little while and I'll get you something." So she took a basket and started out to the storehouse. This storehouse was built upon poles high up from the ground, to keep it out of the reach of animals, and there was a ladder to climb up by, and one door, but no other opening. Every day when Selu got ready to cook the dinner she would go out to the storehouse with a basket and bring it back full of corn and beans. The boys had never been inside the storehouse, so wondered where all the corn and beans could come from, as the house was not a very large one; so as soon as Selu went out of the door the Wild Boy said to his brother, "Let's go and see what she does." They ran around and climbed up at the back of the storehouse and pulled out a piece of clay from between the logs, so that they could look in. There they saw

Selu standing in the middle of the room with the basket in front of her on the floor. Leaning over the basket, she rubbed her stomach – *so* – and the basket was half full of corn. Then she rubbed under her armpits – *so* – and the basket was full to the top with beans. The boys looked at each other and said, "This will never do; our mother is a witch. If we eat any of that it will poison us. We must kill her."

When the boys came back into the house, she knew their thoughts before they spoke. "So you are going to kill me?" said Selu. "Yes," said the boys, "you are a witch." "Well," said their mother, "when you have killed me, clear a large piece of ground in front of the house and drag my body seven times around the circle. Then drag me seven times over the ground inside the circle, and stay up all night and watch, and in the morning you will have plenty of corn." The boys killed her with their clubs, and cut off her head and put it up on the roof of the house with her face turned to the west, and told her to look for her husband. Then they set to work to clear the ground in front of the house, but instead of clearing the whole piece they cleared only seven little spots. This is why corn now grows only in a few places instead of over the whole world. They dragged the body of Selu around the circle, and wherever her blood fell on the ground the corn sprang up. But instead of dragging her body seven times across the ground they dragged it over only twice, which is the reason the Indians still work their crop but twice. The two brothers sat up and watched their corn all night, and in the morning it was full grown and ripe.

When Kana'tĭ came home at last, he looked around, but could not see Selu anywhere, and asked the boys where was their mother. "She was a witch, and we killed her," said the boys; "there is her head up there on top of the house." When he saw his wife's head on the roof, he was very angry, and said, "I won't stay with you any longer; I am going to the Wolf people." So he started off, but before he had gone far the Wild Boy changed himself again to a tuft of down, which fell on Kana'tĭ's shoulder. When Kana'tĭ reached the settlement of the Wolf people, they were holding a council in the townhouse. He went in and sat down with the tuft of bird's down on his shoulder, but he never noticed it. When the Wolf chief asked him his business, he said: "I have two bad boys at home, and I want you to go in seven days from now and play ball against them." Although Kana'tĭ spoke as though he wanted them to play a game of ball, the Wolves knew that he meant for them to go and kill the two boys. They promised to go. Then the bird's down blew off from Kana'tĭ's shoulder, and the smoke carried it up through the hole in the roof of the townhouse. When it came down on the ground outside, the Wild Boy took his right shape again and went home and told his brother all that he had heard in the townhouse. But when Kana'tï left the Wolf people, he did not return home, but went on farther.

The boys then began to get ready for the Wolves, and the Wild Boy – the magician – told his brother what to do. They ran around the house in a wide circle until they had made a trail all around it excepting on the side from which the Wolves would come, where they left a small open space. Then they made four large bundles of arrows and placed them at four different points on the outside of the circle, after which they hid themselves in the woods and waited for the Wolves. In a day or two a whole party of Wolves came and surrounded the house to kill the boys. The Wolves did not notice the trail around the house, because they came in where the boys had left the opening, but the moment they went inside the circle the trail changed to a high brush fence and shut them in. Then the boys on the outside took their arrows and began shooting them down, and as the Wolves could not jump over the fence they were all killed, excepting a few that escaped through the opening into a great swamp close by. The boys ran around the swamp, and a circle of fire sprang up in their tracks and set fire to the grass and bushes and burned up nearly all the other Wolves. Only two or three got away, and from these have come all the wolves that are now in the world.

Soon afterward some strangers from a distance, who had heard that the brothers had a wonderful grain from which they made bread, came to ask for some, for none but Selu and her family had ever known corn before. The boys gave them seven grains of corn, which they told them to plant the next night on their way home, sitting up all night to watch the corn, which would have seven ripe ears in the morning. These they were to plant the next night and watch in the same way, and so on every night until they reached home, when they would have corn enough to supply the whole people. The strangers lived seven days' journey away. They took the seven grains and watched all through the darkness until morning, when they saw seven tall stalks, each stalk bearing a ripened ear. They gathered the ears and went on their way. The next night they planted all their corn, and guarded it as before until daybreak, when they found an abundant increase. But the way was long and the sun was hot, and the people grew tired. On the last night before reaching home they fell asleep, and in the morning the corn they had planted had not even sprouted. They brought with them to their settlement what corn they had left and planted it, and with care and attention were able to raise a crop. But ever since the corn must be watched and tended through half the year, which before would grow and ripen in a night.

As Kana'tï did not return, the boys at last concluded to go and find him. The Wild Boy took a gaming wheel and rolled it toward the Darkening land. In a little while the wheel came rolling back, and the boys knew their father was not there. He rolled it to the south and to the north, and each time the wheel came back to him, and they knew their father was not there. Then he rolled it toward the Sunland, and it did not return. "Our father is there," said the Wild Boy, "let us go and find him." So the two brothers set off toward the east, and after traveling a long time they came upon Kana'tï walking along with a little dog by his side. "You bad boys," said their father, "have you come here?" "Yes," they answered, "we always accomplish what we start out to do – we are men." "This dog overtook me four days ago," then said Kana'tï, but the boys knew that the dog was the wheel which they had sent after him to find him. "Well," said Kana'tï, "as you have found me, we may as well travel together, but I shall take the lead."

Soon they came to a swamp, and Kana'tï told them there was something dangerous there and they must keep away from it. He went on ahead, but as soon as he was out of sight the Wild Boy said to his brother, "Come and let us see what is in the swamp." They went in together, and in the middle of the swamp they found a large panther asleep. The Wild Boy got out an arrow and shot the panther in the side of the head. The panther turned his head and the other boy shot him on that side. He turned his head away again and the two brothers shot together – *tust, tust, tust!* But the panther was not hurt by the arrows and paid no more attention to the boys. They came out of the swamp and soon overtook Kana'tï, waiting for them. "Did you find it?" asked Kana'tï. "Yes," said the boys, "we found it, but it never hurt us. We are men." Kana'tï was surprised, but said nothing, and they went on again.

After a while he turned to them and said, "Now you must be careful. We are coming to a tribe called the Anăda'dûñtăskĭ ('Roasters, i.e., cannibals), and if they get you they will put you into a pot and feast on you." Then he went on ahead. Soon the boys came to a tree which had been struck by lightning, and the Wild Boy directed his brother to gather some of the splinters from the tree and told him what to do with them. In a little while they came to the settlement of the cannibals, who, as soon as they saw the boys, came running out, crying, "Good, here are two nice fat strangers. Now we'll have a grand feast!" They caught the boys and dragged them into the townhouse, and sent word to all the people of the settlement to come to the feast. They made up a great fire, put water into a large pot and set it to boiling, and then seized the Wild Boy and put him down into it. His brother was not in the least frightened and made no attempt to escape, but quietly knelt down and began putting the splinters into the fire, as if to make it burn better. When the cannibals thought the meat was about ready they lifted the pot from the fire, and that instant a blinding light filled the townhouse, and the lightning began to dart from one side to the other, striking down the cannibals until not one of them was left alive. Then the lightning went up through the smoke-hole, and the next moment there were the two boys standing outside the townhouse as though nothing had happened. They went on and soon met Kana'tï, who seemed much surprised to see them, and said, "What! are you here again?" "O, yes, we never give up. We are great men!" "What did the cannibals do to you?" "We met them and they brought us to their townhouse, but they never hurt us." Kana'tï said nothing more, and they went on.

*   *   *   *   *   *   *

He soon got out of sight of the boys, but they kept on until they came to the end of the world, where the sun comes out. The sky was just coming down when they got there, but they waited until it went up again, and then they went through and climbed up on the other side. There they found Kana'tï and Selu sitting together. The old folk received them kindly and were glad to see them, telling them they might stay there a while, but then they must go to live where the sun goes down. The boys stayed with their parents seven days and then went on toward the Darkening land, where they are now. We call them "The Little Men," and when they talk to each other we hear low rolling thunder in the west.

*   *   *   *   *   *   *

After Kana'tï's boys had let the deer out from the cave where their father used to keep them, the hunters tramped about in the woods for a long time without finding any game, so that the people were very hungry. At last they heard that the Thunder Boys were now living in the far west, beyond the sun door, and that if they were sent for they could bring back the game. So they sent messengers for them, and the boys came and sat down in the middle of the townhouse and began to sing.

At the first song there was a roaring sound like a strong wind in the northwest, and it grew louder and nearer as the boys sang on, until at the seventh song a whole herd of deer, led by a large buck, came out from the woods. The boys had told the people to be ready with their bows and arrows, and when the song was ended and all the deer were close around the townhouse, the hunters shot into them and killed as many as they needed before the herd could get back into the timber.

Then the Thunder Boys went back to the Darkening land, but before they left they taught the people the seven songs with which to call up the deer. It all happened so long ago that the songs are now forgotten – all but two, which the hunters still sing whenever they go after deer.

SENECA (A)

Indian myths about the origin of the earth, or of the emergence of a particular people, offer their listeners (who may subsequently be retellers) a way of assessing the appropriateness of tribal practices to natural conditions. The beginning of the Seneca world is here imagined as resulting from acts of a primordial sky people who adhere to the ancient Seneca cultural practice of treating dreams as warnings of disasters that will certainly occur – unless the dreamer tells others of the dream and together they take action, doing whatever the dream has implied will avert the threatened evil. This is why the sky people uproot the tree for the benefit of the afflicted woman. But Seneca listeners would have understood as fully as we the validity of the young man's anger at the destruction of the tree on which his people depend for their food. Thus, like a great many Native American "origin myths," this one begins by provoking an ethical dilemma created by long-established practices and beliefs. For the Seneca and other Indians there is no authoritarian Old Testament God who lays down absolute and historically unconditional laws. For Native Americans, "the" beginning is as dynamically problematic as the changing forms of the natural environment and their culture, which derives from and is sustained by sacred nature.

For the Seneca, their humanity begins not in claiming dominion over the earth but in recognizing that it originated in and, was nurtured by what the Judeo-Christian tradition treats as inferior beings, brutes. This "origin" story evokes intensified awareness of both the physical and ethical complexities of a culture whose foundation is inseparable from natural processes from its beginning to the present instant. So the opening scene foreshadows the subsequent development of human life on earth as one that emerges from conflict. The fierce battle between the opposed energies of the human twins contrasts spectacularly with the generous reception by birds and animals of the falling woman and the life-nurturing powers of earth, water, and wind. Into this benign yet dynamic environment, Flint and Sprout reintroduce the conflict of the sky-people in a manner which shapes in a new way the physical environment in which the Seneca must live. This is a narrative of the "emergence" of human consciousness as "disturbing" – for good or ill – all natural processes. It presents its audience with the opposite of dogmatic truth or definitive commandments for behavior. Instead it provokes self-awareness of the dangerous potency of human powers to affect the natural world, home to a multitude of interrelated beings and therefore a place where the deepest wisdom is learning adaptability to circumstances that are always changing because they are continuously renewing themselves.

9

From Jeremiah Curtin and J. N. B. Hewitt, *Seneca Fiction, Legends, and Myths*. Annual Report of the Bureau of American Ethnology 32 (1910–11), 460–1.

A long time ago human beings lived high up in what is now called heaven. They had a great and illustrious chief.

It so happened that this chief's daughter was taken very ill with a strange affliction. All the people were very anxious as to the outcome of her illness. Every known remedy was tried in an attempt to cure her, but none had any effect.

Near the lodge of this chief stood a great tree, which every year bore corn used for food. One of the friends of the chief had a dream, in which he was advised to tell the chief that in order to cure his daughter he must lay her beside this tree, and that he must have the tree dug up. This advice was carried out to the letter. While the people were at work and the young woman lay there, a young man came along. He was very angry and said: "It is not at all right to destroy this tree. Its fruit is all that we have to live on." With this remark he gave the young woman who lay there ill a shove with his foot, causing her to fall into the hole that had been dug.

Now, that hole opened into this world, which was then all water, on which floated waterfowl of many kinds. There was no land at that time. It came to pass that as these waterfowl saw this young woman falling they shouted, "Let us receive her," whereupon they, at least some of them, joined their bodies together, and the young woman fell on this platform of bodies. When these were wearied they asked, "Who will volunteer to care for this woman?" The great Turtle then took her, and when he got tired of holding her, he in turn asked who would take his place. At last the question arose as to what they should do to provide her with a permanent resting place in this world. Finally it was decided to prepare the earth, on which she would live in the future. To do this it was determined that soil from the bottom of the primal sea should be brought up and placed on the broad, firm carapace of the Turtle, where it would increase in size to such an extent that it would accommodate all the creatures that should be produced thereafter. After much discussion the toad was finally persuaded to dive to the bottom of the waters in search of soil. Bravely making the attempt, he succeeded in bringing up soil from the depths of the sea. This was carefully spread over the carapace of the Turtle, and at once both began to grow in size and depth.

After the young woman recovered from the illness from which she suffered when she was cast down from the upper world, she built herself a shelter, in which she lived quite contentedly. In the course of time she brought forth a girl baby, who grew rapidly in size and intelligence.

When the daughter had grown to young womanhood, the mother and she were accustomed to go out to dig wild potatoes. Her mother had said to her that in doing this she must face the West at all times. Before long the young daughter gave signs that she was about to become a mother. Her mother reproved her, saying that she had violated the injunction not to face the east, as her condition showed that she had faced the wrong way while digging potatoes. It is said that the breath of the West Wind had entered her person, causing conception. When the days of her delivery were at hand, she overheard twins within her body in a hot debate as to which should be born first and as to the proper place of exit, one declaring that he was going to emerge through the armpit of his mother, the other saying that he would emerge in the natural way. The first one born, who was of a reddish color, was called Othagwenda; that is, Flint. The other, who was light in color, was called Djuskaha; that is, the Little Sprout.

The grandmother of the twins liked Djuskaha and hated the other; so they cast Othagwenda into a hollow tree some distance from the lodge.

The boy that remained in the lodge grew very rapidly, and soon was able to make himself bows and arrows and to go out to hunt in the vicinity. Finally, for several days he returned home without his bow and arrows. At last he was asked why he had to have a new bow and arrows every morning. He replied that there was a young boy in a hollow tree in the neighborhood who used them. The grandmother inquired where the tree stood, and he told her; whereupon then they went there and brought the other boy home again.

When the boys had grown to man's estate, they decided that it was necessary for them to increase the size of their island, so they agreed to start out together, afterward separating to create forests and lakes and other things. They parted as agreed, Othagwenda going westward and Djuskaha eastward. In the course of time, on returning, they met in their shelter or lodge at night, then agreeing to go the next day to see what each had made. First they went west to see what Othagwenda had made. It was found that he had made the country all rocks and full of ledges, and also a mosquito which was very large. Djuskaha asked the mosquito to run, in order that he might see whether the insect could fight. The mosquito ran, and sticking his bill through a sapling, thereby made it fall, at which Djuskaha said, "That will not be right, for you would kill the people who are about to come." So, seizing him, he rubbed him down in his hands, causing him to become very small; then he blew on the mosquito, whereupon he flew away. He also modified some of the other animals which his brother had made. After returning to their lodge, they agreed to go the next day to see what Djuskaha had fashioned. On visiting the east the next day, they found that Djuskaha had made a large number of animals which were so fat that they could hardly move; that he had made the sugar-maple trees to drop syrup; that he had made the sycamore tree to bear fine fruit; that the rivers were so formed that half the water flowed upstream and the other half downstream. Then the reddish-colored brother, Othagwenda, was greatly displeased with what his brother had made, saying that the people who were about to come would live too easily and be too happy. So he shook violently the various animals – the bears, deer, and turkeys – causing them to become small at once, a characteristic which attached itself to their descendants. He also caused the sugar maple to drop sweetened water only, and the fruit of the sycamore to become small and useless; and lastly he caused the water of the rivers to flow in only one direction, because the original plan would make it too easy for the human beings who were about to come to navigate the streams.

The inspection of each other's work resulted in a deadly disagreement between the brothers, who finally came to grips and blows, and Othagwenda was killed in the fierce struggle.

SENECA (B)

This story illustrates how intertextuality functions in cultures without writing, especially how native tellers make use of significant motifs in foundational myths. This account of incestuous impulse a Seneca audience would instantly perceive as alluding to the preceding myth (story 9). Could the sister accept (as she is asked to) that her brother is two persons, there would be no threat of incest, no need for condemnation of "the friend." But that would overturn the origin myth's rejection of ethical equality between the opposed twins: constructive Sprout is good, destructive Flint is bad for people and the environment. The brother's claim to psychological innocence is invalid, even though the truth of his split personality is represented so vividly as to arouse our sympathy. This ambivalence the storyteller uses to reveal the condemnation of incest as rooted in something deeper than arbitrary kinship rules.[1] The taboo is shown to reinforce the primary structural principle of the natural world, which derives from Sprout's defeat of his destructive twin, whom he wished to befriend. The Seneca ethical system thus reflects the fundamental order of nature. A modern reader impressed by the acuteness of Seneca psychological insight might consider that its source lies in the Seneca grounding their ethics in the complexity of natural processes, which can make nothing closer together (twin siblings) than what has to be unalterably distinguished.

---

1 In many Indian societies (of which the Seneca are one) with strong clan organization, "brother" or "sister" might refer to members of the same clan and generation as well as to genetic siblings.

10

From Arthur C. Parker, *Seneca Myths and Folk Tales*. Buffalo, NY: Buffalo Historical Society, Publication Series 27 (1923), 290–2.

There was a lodge in the forest where very few people ever came, and there dwelt a young man and his sister. The youth was unlike other persons for one half of his head had hair of a reddish cast, while the other side was black.

He used to leave his sister in the lodge and go away on long hunting trips. On one occasion the young woman, his sister, saw, so she thought, her brother coming down the path to the lodge. "I thought you just went away to hunt," said the sister. "Oh, I thought I would come back," said he.

Then he sat down on the bed with the sister and embraced her and acted as a lover. The sister reproached him and said that she was very angry. But again he endeavored to fondle her in a familiar way, but again was repulsed. This time he went away.

The next day the brother returned and found his sister very angry. She would scarcely speak to him, though hitherto she had talked a great deal.

"My sister," said he. "I am at loss to know why you treat me thus. It is not your custom."

"Oh you ought to know that you have abused me," said the girl.

"I never abused you. What are you talking about?" he said.

"Oh you know that you embraced me in an improper way yesterday," said the sister.

"I was not here yesterday," asserted the youth. "I believe that my friend who resembles me in every respect has been here."

"You have given a poor excuse," replied his sister. "I hope your actions will not continue."

Soon the brother went away again, stating that he would be absent three days. In a short time the sister saw, as she thought, a figure looking like her brother skulking in the underbrush. His shirt and leggings were the same as her brother's and his hair was the same. So then she knew that her brother had returned for mischief. Soon he entered the lodge and embraced her, and this time in anger she tore his cheeks with her nails and sent him away.

In three days the brother returned with a deer, but his sister would not speak to him. Said he, "My sister, I perceive that you are angry at me. Has my friend been here?"

It was some time before the sister replied, and then she wept, saying, "My brother, you have abused me and I scratched your face. I perceive that it is still torn by my finger nails."

"Oh, my face," laughed the brother. "My face was torn by thorns as I hunted deer. If you scratched my friend that is the reason I am scratched. Whatever happens to either one of us happens to the other." But the sister would not believe this.

Again the brother went on a hunting trip, and again the familiar figure returned. This time the sister tore his hunting shirt from the throat down to the waistline. Moreover she threw a ladle of hot bear grease on the shirt. This caused his quick departure.

Returning in due time the brother brought in his game and threw it down. Again the sister was angry and finally accused him. Pointing to his grease-smeared torn shirt she said that this was evidence enough.

"Oh my sister," explained the brother. "I tore my shirt on a broken limb as I climbed a tree after a raccoon. In making soup from bear meat I spilled it on my shirt." Still the sister refused to believe him.

"Oh my sister," said the brother, in distressed tones. "I am greatly saddened to think you will not believe me. My friend looks exactly as I do, and whatever happens to him happens to me. I shall now be compelled to find my friend and bring him to you and when I do I shall be compelled to kill him before you for his evil designs upon you. If you would believe me nothing evil would befall us, but I now think I myself shall die."

The sister said nothing for she would not believe her brother.

The brother now began to pile up dried meat and to repair the lodge. He then went out into the forest without his bow and arrows, and in a short time returned with another man exactly resembling him, and whose clothing was spotted and torn in a similar way. Leading him to the lodge fire he began to scold him in an angry manner. "You have betrayed me and abused my sister," he said. "Now is the time for you to die." Taking out an arrow from a quiver he cast it into the heart of his double and killed him. The sister saw her assailant fall to the floor, and then looked up as she heard her brother give a war cry and fall as dead with blood streaming from a wound in his chest over his heart.

ESKIMO

Nothing is more baffling to the modern reader than Native American thought and feeling about animals – and a high proportion of Native American stories are about animals. Every minute of each Indian's life was spent in intimate contact with an environment virtually unaffected by human activities. The survival of each individual and every Indian culture depended on continual keen attention to every kind of natural phenomena. The foundation of Indian understanding of their world was their belief that it was their proper home and equally the proper home of every other living thing. Of course they disliked being pestered by mosquitoes and blackflies, and they pulled off ticks and leeches, but without our feelings of resentment. Mosquitoes, flies, and ticks are parts of an enormously diversified world in which all creatures pursue their own purposes and functions, their collaborations and competitions manifesting the unceasing interchanging of energies that is the enduring life of the world – a life Indians delighted in and found a source of unfailing interest.

Indians did not, like us, regard themselves as the world's master species. Observations taught them that other species (what they called "people") were commonly better equipped with attributes like fur coats to survive climatological rigors. At the climax of Sioux Plains culture founded on buffalo hunting in the early nineteenth century, the various Siouan bands probably numbered some tens of thousands in country inhabited by sixty million buffalo. Indians carefully avoided poisonous snakes like water moccasins and rattlers, but they never killed them simply because they were dangerous. Indians were deeply upset when whites wantonly killed such "vermin" – for which there is no equivalent word in any Indian language.

Indians regarded animals like cougars, wolves, and bears with respect but not fear. I have never encountered an Indian story of an unprovoked attack by such animals on humans. Indians knew the danger of inadvertently getting between a mother bear and her cubs, but if a woman encountered a bear in a berry patch (not an uncommon occurrence) she spoke quietly to it and slowly backed away. Indians spoke to animals because they assumed that each species had its own system of communication by which individuals passed information back and forth. Observing that animals acted consistently and displayed intelligence in their behavior, Indians adopted the view that one got along best with other creatures by attributing to them capacities equivalent of those that make possible our cultures. This view facilitates understanding of the complex interplay of reciprocality and competition that constitutes any ecological system. Nowhere was that interplay of more concern to Indians than in their hunting.

In all aboriginal North American cultures hunting was a significant food resource. Most men from early boyhood trained themselves as hunters, devoting years to honing their skills at making and using weapons, studying animal behavior, and improving their stalking skills. Yet Native American hunters invariably credited their success not to their abilities but to the spontaneous willingness of quarry to offer themselves as prey. Animals would not offer themselves if a hunter violated the reciprocity between culture and nature expressed by his adherence to formalized behavioral practices in preparing to hunt (fasting or sexual abstinence, for example), in the hunting actions themselves, and in his treatment of the animal after it was slain. The release of an arrow was often accompanied by a formal prayer. Ritual acts of gratitude were commonly performed after a kill. The logic of these procedures is that, although a hunter usually operated alone, his only reason for killing game was for the survival of his family and tribe, his people. Hunting was a cultural activity affecting the ecological wholeness with which not only human and animal individuals were concerned but also their species-peoples.

In this Eskimo story the protagonist fails as a hunter because he eats without attention to the condition and actions around him of the women upon which the welfare of the community depends just as much as upon his hunting. Provoked by Mountain-Woman to rid himself of his faults of cultural inattention, he fails in the opposite way by falling in love with his prey. He violates the interdependence of hunter and quarry founded on their difference. His personal affection, ultimately reciprocated by the "little wife," is incompatible with the mutual respect for distinctions which is the basis for the ecological balance between human hunters and animal prey. Successful hunting depends equally on respect for those of one's kind who do not hunt and for the special integrity of what is hunted. Such respect alone makes possible the generosity of animals willing to give up some of their lives to sustain human lives. The story fosters appreciation of the responsibility of every lone hunter to maintain his culture's role in the ecological wholeness of the natural world.

11

From *In Honor of Eyak: The Art of Anna Nelson Harry*, ed. Michael E. Krauss. Fairbanks, AL: Native Language Center, University of Alaska (1982), 120–2. Reprinted by permission of the Native Language Center.

Two men were trappers. One of them kept catching a lot of groundhogs; he kept bringing in lots of groundhogs. The other man, though, never caught anything, anything at all.

As he was camped out on a trapping expedition, Mountain-Woman came upon him. His companion had gone home without him. Mountain-Woman went up to him and said," Do you know why you don't catch anything?"

"No."

"You eat while women comb their hair. While women tidy up babies, you eat. That's why you never catch anything at all."

Then he said, "What will become of me, what I shall I do? I have nothing."

"If you would listen to what I'm telling you, you would understand why you never catch anything. While women who are having their periods clean themselves, you eat." She poked him in the back with her staff. Then all those things, women's hair, children's excrement, menstrual blood, all those things spewed out from inside him.

Then she told him, "Tomorrow get up early and go to your traps." She went away. He ate nothing and went to sleep. As it was getting light towards the south, he got up. He went among his traps. Almost all his traps were full of groundhogs.

One of the groundhogs was white, pure snow-white. He fell in love with her. As he was carrying them along in a pack on his back, it burst, and all the groundhogs immediately escaped., running off in all directions. Mountain Woman had warned him that he would catch a white groundhog, and that he must free her. That was the one he chased, the snow-white one. Just as she was running into her hole, he caught hold of her tail. He hung on to her tail, and it broke off in his hand. He stayed right there.

Pretty soon a girl came out to him from where the groundhog has run in. She said, "Give it back to me, my younger sister's ribbon. Give me back my younger sister's ribbon."

"I won't give it back to you. Tell her she must come out here."

"She doesn't want to come out here. You pulled that ribbon off her head. That's why."

"Then couldn't I go in there with you?"

"If you'll give it back to her, you may come on in with me." Way at the back of that little place she sat, that younger sister, weeping for her ribbon.

So he went up to her and said, "I'll give it back to you." He was quite in love with her. "I'll give it back to you, your ribbon, if you'll live with me."

Then the older sister said to her, "Live with him. It would never do for you to go around without your ribbon." That is how he married her.

He was gone for a whole year, passing the winter there. As spring came, at the time groundhogs come out of their holes, he came out. In his own eyes he was still a person. As far as he knew he was a regular human.

Then some people came along in their boat down below, and as they were passing by he yelled down to them. But what came out was a whistle. He was whistling at them. He then realized what had happened to him. He looked at his hands, and they were groundhog's. The back of his hands, groundhog's. He looked at his feet, groundhog's. He was becoming a groundhog. He ran back in. Already he was turning into a groundhog, a whistler.

Then the people found out about him. The real people found out that the man who was missing had turned into a groundhog. They went to get him back.

One evening the little groundhog-wife went out and the people sneaked up on her. Two of them grabbed that girl. They seized her and carried her off. That little groundhog-girl was human in their eyes. The husband ran along after his little wife. So he too was captured. Captured, he said, "Give me back my little wife. Don't take her from me."

"Come with us and we'll give her back to you." He went with them.

He went with them and rejoined his own people. but he didn't any longer eat what people eat. He ate only what groundhogs eat. Shieldfern-sprouts is what he ate. But whatever his own people gave him he would not eat. He would just stow it away in back, behind him.

Then his little wife sneaked away. She got away and ran home while it was dark and he was asleep. She got away early. "Where is she? What have you done with her, my little wife?"

"We don't know what happened. Maybe she ran back home." She had gone home. He went after her, looking for her. He found her home. Because she had gone back to her own kind, her husband wasn't happy with her any more.

But that little wife was carrying and bore a child. It was half human. About half of it was a person. The lower half was groundhog, and toward the head was human. This made him really understand. "I guess I really must be a groundhog. They have made me one of them." That's what he said to himself. "I suppose I may as well stay right here with them."

Winter was coming again then, and already there was snow. There was a lot of snow. What did he go out for? He went out with her child. It isn't told whether it was a boy or a girl. Anyway, it was their child. It was snowing some.

Then from way up above where he had gone out with child, before he realized what was happening, the snow started to slide down, a snowslide. He was buried in that avalanche and died. He died, and the child died with him.

He was dead when some people came along hunting. They were after porcupines. They saw the snowslide that had taken him down with the child. Where the snowslide wasn't too deep they split some trees and fashioned them into shovels. With those they dug them out. Then they saw that the child he had was about half groundhog. But only his hands and feet were groundhog. Also his nose and mouth were getting like a groundhog's, and his whiskers had grown long.

That wife had been looking for him, looking for her husband. She was saying, "He's been buried in an avalanche with my little child. There's been an avalanche." Her child was dead.

Then her older sister said, to her, "Why did you let him take the child out?" "I didn't think this would happen to him," she answered. "What will become of us?" she asked her older sister. "There's not just one man. Your relatives are many. Your own kind are here. There are many groundhogs." "Never. When I die, I'll die. My little child is dead."

Then she went away from there, from her older sister. From a summit way up there she hurled herself down. She fell rolling down from the mountaintop, a long way, into the deep snow, she too. So she too died.

Their story goes only that far. That's all.

CHEROKEE (C)

Stories told by Native Americans reveal they conceived of the natural cosmos as never static but a perpetual interactivity of diverse energies. All elements of the world were always moving in a condition of dynamic interdependence, continuously changing and being changed. In form and theme Indian stories reflect this conception. They aim for a wholeness that encourages retellings and which does not depend on absolute closure but embodies the ever-flowing continuity of vital energies. Thematically, as in this hunting story, transformation, reciprocity, and reversal are characteristically principal concerns. During a communal hunt a lone scout sees a strange old man with a skin of stone and a magic cane for locating his prey – which is human hunters. The scout wisely takes no personal action but returns to his people to report. Against the seemingly invulnerable cannibal, a totally desocialized person, the community defends itself with its weakest members. The menstruating women are the antithesis of Dressed-in-Stone. His strength is external, skin become flint that insulates him from his kind, whose real strength is their inner "weakness": the downward flow of menstrual blood manifests the capacity of women to create more life. Confronted by the vulnerability of vitality, Dressed-in-Stone vomits up blood and finally falls before the woman whose first period is beginning. Cooked by transforming fire, the cannibal's voice reveals cures for sickness and songs that assure killing of game. Finally his alienated humanity is entirely retransformed into soft paint, the color of blood, spread on the body's surface to facilitate realization of the inner desires of each individual within the community he had hunted.

12

From James Mooney, *Myths of the Cherokee*. Washington, DC: Annual Report of the Bureau of American Ethnology 19 (1897–8), 3–557, 319.

Once when all the people of the settlement were out in the mountains on a great hunt, one man who had gone on ahead climbed to the top of a high ridge and found a large river on the other side. While he was looking across he saw an old man walking on the opposite ridge with a cane that seemed to be made of some bright, shining rock. The hunter watched and saw that every little while the old man would point his cane in a certain direction, then draw it back and smell the end of it. At last he pointed it in the direction of the hunting camp on the other side of the mountain, and this time when he drew back the staff he sniffed it several times as if it smelled very good, and then he started along the ridge straight toward the camp. He moved very slowly, with the help of the cane, until he reached the edge of the ridge, when he threw the cane out into the air and it became a bridge of shining rock stretching across the river. After he had crossed over upon the bridge it became a cane again, and the old man picked it up and started over the mountain toward the camp.

The hunter was frightened, and felt sure it meant mischief, so he hurried down the mountain and took the shortest trail back to the camp to get there before the old man. When he got there and told his story the medicine-man said the old man was a wicked cannibal monster called Dressed-in-Stone, who lived in that part of the country, and was always going about the mountains looking for some hunter to kill and eat. It was very hard to escape from him, because his stick guided him like a dog, and it was nearly as hard to kill him, because his whole body was covered with a skin of solid rock. If he came he would kill and eat them all, and there was only one way to save themselves. He could not bear to look upon a menstrual woman, and if they could find seven menstrual women to stand in the path as he came along the sight would kill him.

So they asked among all the women, and found seven who were sick in that way, and with one of them it had just begun. By the order of the medicine-man they stripped themselves and stood along the path where the old man would come. Soon they heard Dressed-in-Stone coming through the woods, feeling his way with his stone cane. He came along the trail to where the first woman was standing, and as soon as he saw her he started and cried out, "Yu! my grandchild; you are in a very bad state!" He hurried past her, but in a moment he met the next woman, and cried out again, "Yu! my child; you are in a terrible way," and hurried past her, but now he was vomiting blood. He hurried on and met the third and fourth and the fifth woman, but with each one that he saw his step grew weaker until when he came to the last one, with whom the sickness had just begun, the blood poured from his mouth and he fell down on the trail.

Then the medicine-man drove seven sourwood stakes through his body and pinned him to the ground, and when night came they piled great logs over him and set fire to them, and all the people gathered around to see. Dressed-in-Stone had much power and knew many secrets, and now as the fire came close to him he began to talk, and told them the medicine for all kinds of sickness. At midnight he began to sing, and sang the hunting songs for calling up the bear and the deer and all the animals of the woods and mountains. As the blaze grew hotter his voice sank lower and lower, until at last when daylight came, the logs were a heap of white ashes and the voice was silent.

Then the medicine-man told them to rake off the ashes, and where the body had lain they found only a large lump of red paint and a magic stone. He kept the stone for himself and calling the people around him he painted them, on the face and breast, with the red paint, and whatever each person prayed for while the painting was being done – whether for hunting success, for working skill, or for a long life – that gift was his.

TRICKSTER

Ubiquitous in Native American storytelling although absent from our literature, the "trickster figure" is not a character but a figure of speech, a trope. Trickster is a modality of spoken discourse: he facilitates the special sociability made possible by language. Unlike bees, ants, and all other social creatures, humans form societies that empower the uniqueness of each of their members. Language makes it possible for humans to form communities that are strong because they encourage individualization. The infinite flexibility of linguistic intercommunication permits productive use even of the mistakes and confusions we make in speaking to one another. Human language transcends every other semiotic system because it can exploit to positive effect possibilities that are only imagined, can correct its own errors, and can continually extend its scope and refine its precision. The pleasure people take in puzzles, riddles, ambiguities, ironies, absurdities, nonsense, and paradoxes testifies to the potential of language to expand and reconfigure itself. This unique power enables it to enhance and subtilize interrelationships among members of any social-linguistic group. This advantage of dependence of social relations upon language is made manifest in the rhetorical figure of trickster.

Our insatiable delight in laughing together with others is nurtured in trickster stories. Native American peoples imagined the trickster trope in a plenitude of forms, all simultaneously human and animal, as a person-fox, person-spider, person-raven, person-rabbit, but most often as a person-coyote, shifty, fast-moving, foolishly ingenious and trouble-making for both himself and others. In whatever form, the trickster speech figure unites spoken language with modes of what Mikhail Bakhtin called "translinguistic communication" – all the bodily processes which affect social relationships, from touching, patting, caressing, stroking, gripping, pushing, kicking, and tickling, to those personal expulsions such as breathing, humming, belching, farting, pissing, defecating, vomiting, and crying by which we physically impinge upon the physical existence of our fellows even as they impinge upon us. Trickster unites oral linguistic and bodily translinguistic interactions to create carnivalesque enjoyment of common features of everyday life. This enjoyment includes a testing, subverting, even inverting of social arrangements we have internalized for our satisfaction and benefit, but sometimes to our inconvenience. Trickster figures forth shared self-awareness of these internalizations. At this awareness's highest intensity the verbal story explodes in joint laughter that refreshes each mind. Upon such refreshed self-consciousness depends our power of **generating** ever-more effective modes of productive social interdependence.

Modern readers are often baffled by trickster stories, because our written literature has almost entirely lost the capacity of Indian oral storytelling for exploring imaginable impossibilities in normal life. These begin with the trickster figure of speech operating **simultaneously** as human and animal. "He" is a dramatic paradox, like every paradox revealing the conceptual limits of both our social and linguistic systems that define the character of the community in which we live. By transgressing these limits, narratively articulating what is "impossible," trickster liberates our imaginations to discover the structure of our mindset. That mindset, not nature, is responsible for what to us is possible, that is, what is real. Understanding this, we can comprehend why Indians were so fond of trickster stories; as a Navajo said, they make all things possible.

THREE CHINOOK-WISHRAM
COYOTE TALES

Contemporary readers may penetrate the strangeness of trickster stories by regarding them as "thought experiments" which isolate a slice of social reality to dramatize some ethical problem. Narrowness of focus allows exaggerated motivations and fantastic behavior to make visible contradictions (both social and psychological) embedded in our institutionalized practices. Thus the women from whom the fish are liberated seem less selfish than Coyote gobbling the food of those who generously (if unwisely) saved and fed him. The women are the possibility of humanity to be realized in the Wishram people who are about to appear: what the women *are* now doing **will** become hoarding needed food. Coyote, the bestower of fish, exhibits a deceitfulness and greedy selfishness, but also breaks four of his five digging sticks in creating the new channel. Good but difficult work is sometimes done by unattractive people. To take responsibility for reconfiguring our physical environment is no easy task, and may require qualities not easily reconciled with the conventional decencies. Coyote knows what it is to be hungry, and does his digging not for self-aggrandizement but for the Wishram's benefit. So it is appropriate that he finally identifies the women as the swallows who every spring accompany the returning salmon, the Wishram's primary food.

The laughter evoked even in "serious" trickster stories (Coyote with half a fish hanging out of his mouth) testifies to their engagement with bodily experience, especially pleasurable or painful emotions. Trickster may arouse diverse, even antithetical, feelings because he is never to be identified with any fixed state of being: he can appear anywhere doing anything – "I am walking about without particular purpose," says Wishram Coyote. Because he is a figure of speech in oral discourse, what he says is what happens. Although words are ephemeral, their sound *waves dying in our ears as we hear, words can constitute and change both physical and cultural actualities. Wishram Coyote establishes a culture that is the physical landscape of the Columbia River, because upon that piece of nature are superimposed systemized ideas and practices of persons who simultaneously occupy physical and cultural space. No Indian culture exists detached from a particular natural situation, which is lived in with such attentive care and continuous awareness as to become a portion of the earth that gives physical coherence to the infinite variety of Wishram thoughts and emotions. In this place laughter, expressive of joyful release from fear, embodies the positiveness of culture's imaginative reconfiguring (rather than transcending) physical realities, bodily and topographical.*

Most trickster stories are funny and told for fun – a sign of their power, dangerous as dynamite. The scandalous merriment of the story about Coyote as medicine man is partly accessible even to a modern reader, because there is some common human nature that can respond to what is unpleasant, nasty, vile. By breaking all the Wishram's social rules Trickster makes them realize how valuable their rules are. The decent covering of thoughtless, automatic behavior Coyote rips from respectful and responsible actions of politeness, whose raison d'être is made apparent by his unrestrained selfish lustfulness. Storytelling arouses self-consciousness and social awareness. Coyote succeeds in fingering the genitals of five sisters because none tells what Coyote has done, and the mother judges that if her daughter keeps quiet about Coyote's behavior he will have "done well to her." Humor makes super-apparent what conventionally is politely unnoticed or concealed. Things like the old man's sensational penis that surpasses even those in Aristophanes' plays conveys the pleasure of awful truths even today, but we miss its peculiar sharpness for the Wishram. Coyote as medicine man satirizes one of their central healing ceremonies. Only Rabelais in our tradition comes close to the hilarious sacrilege of copulating Coyote signaling the devout: "Sing hard!"

13

From Edward Sapir, *Wishram Texts*. Publications of the American Ethnological Society, Leiden: Brill (1909).

Coyote heard about two women who had fish preserved in a pond. Then he went to them as they were collecting driftwood from the river. He turned himself into a piece of wood trying (to get them to pick him up). He drifted along. But then they did not get hold of him. He went ashore, ran off to way yonder up river, and transformed himself into a boy. He put himself into a cradle, threw himself into the river, and again drifted along. The two women caught sight of him wailing. They thought: "Some people have capsized, and this child is drifting towards us." The younger one thought: "Let us get hold of it." But the older woman did not want to have the child. Now it was drifting along. The older one thought: "That is Coyote." Nevertheless the younger woman took the child and put it in a canoe.

The two women started home towards their house. The child was wailing, and they arrived home with it. They took off the cradle from it and looked closely at it. As it turned out, the child was a boy. The younger one said: "A boy is better than driftwood." And then she went and cut an eel and put its tail in his mouth. Then straightway he sucked at it and ate it all up. She gave him another eel, and again he sucked at it, (eating up) only half. Then he fell asleep, and half the eel was lying in his mouth. The two women said: "He is asleep; now let us go for some more wood."

And then they went far away. He arose and saw them going far off. Then he made himself loose and seized their food. He roasted the fish on a spit; they were done and he ate. He caught sight of the fish, which were their food, in a lake. Then he examined (the lake) carefully, and discovered a spot where it would be easy (to make an outlet from it to the river). "Here I shall make the fish break out (from the lake), and then they will go to the Great River." He made five digging-sticks, made them out of young oak. And then he put them down in that place. He started back home towards their house. Again, just as before, he put himself into the cradle. Again there (in his mouth) lay the eel's tail. Again he fell asleep.

Now the two women arrived. "The boy is sleeping," they said; "very good is the boy, being a great sleeper." And then they retired for the night. Daylight came, the boy was sleeping. Again they went for wood. Again he saw them going far away. Then he got up and took their food. He roasted it on a spit and ate it all up. Then straightway he went to where his digging-sticks were. He took hold of one of his digging-sticks. Then he stuck his digger into the ground; he pulled it out, and the earth was all loosened up; his digging-stick broke. He took hold of another one and again stuck it into the ground. Then he loosened up the earth, and his digger was all broken to pieces. He took hold of another one of his digging-sticks. Again he stuck it into the ground; he loosened the earth all up, and his third digger was all broken to pieces. He took hold of the fourth one; again his digger broke. Now at last he took hold of the fifth and stuck it into the ground; he loosened the earth all up. And then the fish slid over into the Great River.

Now then the older woman bethought herself. She said to her companion: "You said, 'The child is good'; I myself thought, 'That is Coyote.' Now this day Coyote has treated us two badly. I told you, 'Let us not take the child, that is Coyote.' Now we have become poor, Coyote has made us so." Then they went to their house, and he too went to them to their house.

He said to them: "Now by what right, perchance, would you two keep the fish to yourselves? You two are birds, and I shall tell you something. Soon now people will come into this land. Listen!" And the people could be heard "du'lululu" (like thunder rumbling afar). "Now they will come into this land; those fish will be the people's food. Whenever a fish will be caught, you two will come. Your name has become Swallows. Now this day I have done with you; thus I shall call you, 'Swallows.' When the people will come, they will catch fish; and then you two will come, and it will be said of you, 'The swallows have come; Coyote called them so.' Thus will the people say: 'From these two did Coyote take away their fish preserved in a pond; now they have come.'" Thus did Coyote call those two.

14

From Edward Sapir, *Wishram Texts*. Publications of the American Ethnological Society, Leiden: Brill (1909).

A certain old man was sitting in the trail with his penis wrapped about him just like a rope. And then Coyote passed by him and went on a little beyond. He saw some women jumping up and down in the water. And then he thought: "I shall borrow from the old man his penis." He went over to him and said to him: "Friend, would you not lend me your penis?" And then (the man) said to him: "All right, I shall lend it to you." So then (Coyote) took it and carried it along with him. Then he put it on to his own penis.

Then he shoved it under water right where the women were jumping up and down. One of the women jumped up, the penis got between her legs, and it remained stuck a little ways. And then she became ill.

Then the (other) women took hold of her and brought her yonder to shore. They saw that something was sticking to her, but they could do nothing with her; they could not cut it out of her with anything. And then they took hold of her and carried her a little farther away from the water. Coyote was far off across the river, and they dragged him into the water. Coyote shouted: "Split a stone (as knife); with it you will cut it off." They said: "What did some person tell us? He said, 'Cut it off with a stone knife.'" And then they looked for it and found a stone. They split it, and with the same they cut off the (penis) from her. It had run up right into her. That Coyote over yonder cut it all off. Then he turned his penis all back (to himself).

Immediately Coyote went on again; he arrived somewhere, and laid himself down there. Now this woman is sick; they took her with them and straightway carried her (home). They looked for a medicine-man and found the Raven. They said to him: "Now you will treat (her)"; then he assented. He went to treat her; he had consented to do so. And then he doctored and doctored (until) he said: "There is nothing in her body, there is no sickness in her body." Thus did speak the Raven.

And then the people said: "Yonder is a certain Coyote, who is a medicine-man." Then they went and said to him: "What do you think, will you treat her? We have come for you." And then he said: "Well, I could not go so far on foot; there must be five women without husbands. No! five women will have to come for me; they will just carry me on their backs." And then they went and said to five women who had no husbands: "Now you will go and bring the old medicine-man." Coyote yonder split some alder-bark and chewed at it. Then the women came to meet him, and he said to them: "I am sick in my breast." Then he spat; he showed them that what he had spit out was red and pretended that it was blood.

"You will just carry me on your backs so that my head is downward, in order that the blood may slowly go down to the ground. If my head is turned upwards, my mouth will perhaps become filled with blood, (so that) I shall die. It is good that my head be down; (so) I shall not die." One of the women straightway took him on her back; the youngest one carried him first; she carried him with his head turned down. She went along with him. And then straightway he put his hands between her legs. Immediately he stuck his hands into her private parts and fingered them. She thought: "Oh! the old man is bad; the old man did not do good to me." So then she threw him down on the ground. Then he spat blood when she had thrown him down. One of the older sisters spoke, and said to her: "It is not good that you have hurt the old man."

And then one of the women again took him on her back. She went along with him. Straighway again, as before, he treated her; again he put his hands into her private parts. She did not carry him long; she also threw him down. Again one (of the sisters) said to her: "It is not good that you have thrown him down; you have hurt the old man. Look at him; again blood is flowing out of his mouth, he is coughing." And then she also put him on her back; now she was the third to carry him. To her also he did as before; he fingered her private parts. She did not carry him long, but threw him down also. And then again one of the women said to them: "Oh! you have not treated the old man well. Now he is continually spitting out much blood, the blood is flowing out of his mouth; you have hurt him badly."

And then the fourth woman took him on her back. That woman also went along with him. He treated her also as before, fingering her private parts. She also threw him down. Behold, now they were approaching to where the girl was lying sick in the house. Now another one of the women, the oldest of all, – she was their oldest sister, – said to them: "How you have treated the old medicine-man! Look, blood is flowing out of his mouth; now he is close to dying. Why have you done thus to the old man?" The four women said among themselves: "Thus has the old man done to me myself." One again said in like manner: "He fingered my private parts." They said to one another: "Now she too will find out; she will think that the old man is bad, after all."

Now also the other one, the fifth, took him on her back and went along with him. Her also he treated as before. Now the house was near by, and there she threw him down. And then people were gotten where the woman lay sick who should sing for him, while he was to treat (her); they obtained animals of such kind from the land, large deer who could make much noise; they were to sing out loud.

Coyote, the medicine-man, said: "Now lay her down carefully." And then they laid her down; the people who were to sing for him seated themselves. The medicine-man said: "I alone would treat her. Put something around her here to hide her from view, so that I may treat her well." And then they took rushes and put them over her to hide her from view. Now there he sat by her, and said to them: "If I turn my hand up, then you shall sing."

Then he took up the song, and they started in singing. And then he treated (her); he spread apart her legs. He stuck his penis into her and copulated with her. She called out: "The old one is copulating with me." He put up his hand and said to them: "Now go ahead, sing hard." And then hard they sang and sang. The two (parts of the) penis stuck together. Truly, that was the same penis which they had cut off with the stone knife; that (Coyote) penetrated her halfways, thus he copulated with her. The two (parts of the) penis recognized each other, they stuck together.

And then he pulled it out of her. Straightway she became well. Her mother asked her: "How are you feeling now? Have you now become well?" – "Now I have become well, but the old one has copulated with me." – "Well, never mind, just keep quiet; now the old one has done well to you." And then the old man was told: "Now she has become your wife." He said: "I do not want a woman. I am walking about without particular purpose; I desire no woman." Then he went out of the house; he left them.

15

From Edward Sapir, *Wishram Texts*. Publications of the American Ethnological Society, Leiden: Brill (1909).

Telling trickster tales excites productive but at times upsetting reflections on firmly established social conventions: trickster is language bringing into consciousness what has been so taken for granted as to be before unthinkable. Trickster stories often plunge more deeply into unexamined or suppressed portions of our thought and behavior than most of our own literature dares, as is exemplified in this story of mouthless people that provokes imagining our physical capacity to eat, to speak, to tell stories. Trickster persistently reminds us of the physiological foundations of civilized behavior. We cannot live without eating, and the violence of Coyote making the mouth emphasizes the awesome power of speech, which can reorder the natural world. Just as Coyote tore open the earth to produce fish as human food, here the capacity for eating and speech is released by his use of a stone as a knife. In imagining a human function for a natural object he reveals the origin of artifacts while manifesting their power to transform their makers's being. Analogously, he slashes open the place in the face where he perceives the possibility of a mouth. This realization of a human mouth permitting the transcendence of ostensive communication by human language dramatizes how culture is made out of nature. Self-illustrated by these events is how speech by mouths allows imaginative sharing, a power unconfinable by any natural environment. No aspect of physical existence is immune from the exploitive explorations of trickster figurations of speech – even the physical organ that makes trickster storytelling possible.

Again Coyote travelled up the river. In the water he saw the canoe of a certain person, as it turned out, a man. He saw how (the man) dived into the water. He came up out of the water, his hands holding one sturgeon on that side and one sturgeon on this; he put the sturgeons down in the canoe. Then (Coyote) looked on and saw him count them with his finger, pointing about in the canoe. He thought: "When he dives, I shall take hold of and steal from him one of his sturgeons; let us see what he'll do."

The person dived under water. And then (Coyote) swam towards his canoe. He seized one of his sturgeons. He went and took the person's sturgeon with him, and hid it in the bushes. And then that (Coyote) seated himself there and hid. Then the person came up out of the water into his canoe; he put his sturgeons down in the canoe, again one and one. And then he counted them; again he counted them. Quite silently he counted them; there was (only) one sturgeon in his canoe.

And then he pointed his finger out, first up high, (then) a little lower, again a little lower still, finally a little lower still on the ground. There he pointed, where (Coyote) was sitting. Quite silently (he held) his finger there. (Coyote) tried (to move) to one side, there again was he finger. No matter which way (he moved), there was his finger (pointing) at him, Coyote. Where his finger was (pointed to), there he went straight up to him. Straightway he went to meet him; straightway he came quite close to him.

He kept pointing at him; (Coyote) kept dodging from side to side; the person kept him well in eye. And he also looked at the person; the person was strange in appearance. As it turned out, he had no mouth; he had only a nose and eyes and ears. He spoke to (Coyote) with his nose, but he did not hear him; just deep down in his nose (could be heard): "Den den den den." In fact he was scolding that (Coyote) in this way. Thus he said to him with his nose: "You are not good." Thus the person kept telling him; his heart was dark within him. "But perhaps now this man desires the sturgeon; perhaps he is going to kill me." Thus thought Coyote.

And then the person went back to his canoe. (Coyote) made a fire when he had gone. He gathered some stones and heated them in the fire. And then they all became heated up. He cut the sturgeon in two, cut it all up, and carefully made ready the stones. He laid the sturgeon out on the stones and steamed it; it was entirely done. And then he removed it and laid it down. Then that same man who had no mouth went back to him; he met Coyote as he was eating.

And then he took hold of that good well-done sturgeon. Then thought Coyote: "Wonder what he'll do with it!" He looked at him; he took the good (sturgeon). He just sniffed at the sturgeon, then threw it away. And then Coyote thought: "It is not well." He went and brought the sturgeon back and brushed it clean. Now Coyote is thinking: "What is he going to do with it?" Once again he took hold of it and did with it again as before.

He went up to him and looked at him closely. And then he thought: "I don't know what I shall do to make him a mouth." Secretly he took a flint and chipped it on one side; it became just like a sharp knife. And then he went up to him with the flint secretly in hand and looked at him closely. In vain the man tried to dodge from side to side. Now he put the flint down over his mouth. He sliced it open, and his blood flowed out. He breathed: "Haaaa." He said to him: "Go to the river and wash yourself." When he had come up out of the water, he stopped and spoke to Coyote.

Coyote was spoken to (thus): "You do not seem to have steamed a large sturgeon." And then Coyote said: "Well, you would have killed me; you wanted the sturgeon for yourself. You got after me for the sturgeon." Now the people told one another: "There is a man whose mouth has been made for him." In truth, all the people of that same one village were without mouths. And then they betook themselves to him. He made mouths for all the people of that same one village. He called that same land Nimîcxa'ya. They said to him: "We will give you a woman." He said: "No! I should not care for a woman; I'll not take one."

CLACKAMAS (A)

Here trickster appears as fool, self-injuring bumbler, exemplifying what not to do. His foolishness enables listeners to learn to do better. Here we may learn how better to handle the circumstances of death in the family and the accompanying emotions of grief, guilt, and denial that require (for the benefit of both individual and community) assuaging through institutionalized practices of mourning. Coyote's failure at his suicide attempts evoked by his guilt over his children's deaths reveals the useless excessiveness of such feeling – even when "justified." Coyote does bear responsibility – offering a lesson perhaps too painful to teach some listeners except through the distancing of a story. His failure to restore the children to life when provoked by a bug too unimportant to identify typifies trickster the messer-up, but also reminds us that successful living is dealing with little irritations. What mattered most for Clackamas listeners, however, was imagining Coyote the mythic figure undergoing the deepest feelings of irredeemable personal loss anyone may suffer. Good or bad, foolish or wise, we all die, and we all experience the pain of losing those we deeply love. In that perspective personal imperfections become less important than recognizing that our life is also the life of our community. To the degree that we participate communally, we need not give up experiences of human joy before our death. Well-meaning or deceitful, inept or powerful, trickster Coyote affirms that, for all its dangers, difficulties, and disasters, human life is good – it is to be where "people are enjoying themselves."

16

From Melville Jacobs, "Badger and Coyote were Neighbors," *International Journal of American Linguistics* 24:2 (1958), 106–12. Reprinted by permission of the University of Chicago Press.

Coyote and his five children lived there, four males, one female. Badger was a neighbor there. He had five children all males. Each day all ten children would go here and there. They came back in the evening. And the next day they would go again. Now that is the way they were doing. They would go all over, they traveled about.

Now they reached a village, they stayed up above there, they looked down below at it, they saw where the villagers were playing ball. And as they stayed there and watched, the people (of the village beneath) saw them now. They went to the place there where they played ball. Now the villagers played. When they threw the ball it was just like the sun. Now they stayed there, they watched them playing. Sometimes the ball would drop close by them. Now they quit playing. Then the ten children who were watching went back home, they went to their houses.

The next day then they did not go anywhere. All day long they chatted about that ball. They discussed it. Now their father Badger heard them. He said to his sons, "What is it that you are discussing?" So they told their father. "Yes," they said to him, "we got to a village, and they were playing ball. When the ball went it was just like the sun. We thought that we would go get it." Now then he said to his children, "What do you think about talking this over with Coyote too?" So then they said to Coyote, "What do you think?" He said, "My children should be the first ones to run with the ball, if they bring the ball." Badger said, "No. My children should be the first ones to do if." Coyote said, "No. My children have long bodies, their legs are long. They can run (faster than your children). Your children have short legs." So then he replied to Coyote, "Very well then."

Now the next day they got ready, and they went. They reached there. At that place the oldest son of Coyote went immediately to the spot where the ball might drop. He buried himself at that place (on the playing field). Then the next oldest son buried himself farther on, and another one (the third in age) still farther away. All four sons of Coyote covered themselves with soil on the playing field. The last one farther on at the end was their younger sister. Now the five children of Badger remained on the hill above the ball field, they watched.

Soon afterwards then the people (of that village) came there, they came to play ball. Now they threw the ball to where it fell close by Coyote's oldest son. He seized it. They looked for it, they said, "Coyote's son is hiding it!" He let it go, and they took it, and they played more. Now it dropped close by him there once again. So then he took it, and he ran. The people turned and looked, they saw him running, he was taking the ball. Now they ran in pursuit, they got close to him, he got close to his younger brother, he threw the ball to him. He said to him, "We are dying because of the ball. Give a large chunk of it to our father." His pursuers now caught up to and killed him. Then the other one took it, and he ran too. The people pursued him, he got close to his younger brother. Now they seized him, and he threw it to his younger brother. They killed all four of them. Now only their younger sister held the ball, she ran, she ran and ran, she left them quite a distance behind because she was the fastest runner of them all. She got close to the Badgers. Now as the villagers who pursued seized her she threw the ball to them, she said to them, "Give the biggest portion to our father. We have died because of the ball."

The Badgers took the ball. The first and oldest Badger child dropped it when he picked it up. The next to the oldest took it, he also dropped it when he picked it up. The pursuers got to there, and the people stood there watching the Badger children fumbling the ball. They said, they told them, "So those are the ones who would be taking away the ball!" They laughed at the seemingly clumsy Badger children. They said, "Let it be a little later before we kill them!" Soon now the Badgers kicked at the ground, and wind blew and dust and darkness stood there. Dust covered everything, and the wind blew. Now the Badgers ran, they ran away with the ball. And those people pursued them. They got tired, they got thirsty (from wind and dust) they turned back to their home.

On the other hand the Badgers lay down (because of exhaustion) right there when they had gotten close to their own home. And there they sat. Now they hallooed, they said to their father. "Badger! we left your children far back there!" Now they hallooed again, they went and told Coyote, "Back yonder we left your children." That is the way they did to them. Now Badger went outside, he said to his children, "Now really why did you do like that? You have been teasing and paining Coyote." Then the Badger children went downhill and entered the village house, it was only Badger's children who returned. They brought the ball with them.

Now Coyote tried in vain to drown himself. He did not die. Then he built a fire, he made a big fire, he leaped into it there. He did not burn, he did not die. He took a rope, he tied it, he tied it on his throat, he pulled himself up, once more he did not die. He took a knife, he cut his throat, he did not die. He did every sort of thing for killing himself. He gave up. I do not know how many days he was doing like that. Now he quit it, and he merely wept all the day long. After a while he gave that up too.

Then Badger said to his children, "He has quit mourning now. So then cut up the ball for him. Give him half." And they did that for him, they gave him half. He took it, and he went here and there at the place where his children used to play. There he now mashed into many pieces that ball, at the place where they used to play. That was where he took it, he mashed it up, the ball was entirely gone.

Then they continued to live there, and Coyote was all alone. Now he went to work, he made a loose big pack basket. Then it was getting to be springtime, and when the leaves were coming out, now he got ready, and he went to the place where they had killed his children. He got to the grave of his oldest son. He picked ferns, he lined his pack basket with them. He got to the place where they had killed the first of his sons, he collected his bones, he put them into the basket, he laid them in it neatly. Then he got more ferns, he picked the leaves, he covered the bones of his son. Now he went a little farther, and he again got to bones of his second son. Then he also put them into the basket, and that is the way he did again. He collected the bones of all five of his children.

Now he went on, he proceeded very very slowly, he went only a short distance. Then he camped overnight. The next day he proceeded again, also very slowly like that. On the fifth day, then he heard them talking to one another in the basket. They said, "You are lying upon me. Move a little." Then he went along all the more slowly. Now he kept going, he went just a short distance, and then he picked more leaves, he covered it all with utmost care and constant replenishing with fresh leaves. And that is the way he did as he went along.

She (perhaps a centipede) would run across his path, she would say to him, "Sniff sniff sniff! Coyote is taking dead persons along!" He paid no heed to her. Now she ran repeatedly and all the more in front of him, again she would speak like that to him, "Sniff! Coyote is carrying dead persons along!" He laid his basket down very very slowly, he got a stick, he ran after her. I do not know where she went and hid.

Then he packed his carrying basket on his back again, and now he went very very slowly, and he heard his children. Now they were chatting, they were saying, "Move around slowly and carefully! we are making our father tired." Then he was glad, and he went along even more slowly and cautiously. He walked so very slowly that he saw his previous night's campfire, and then he again camped overnight.

He went on again the next morning, and then that thing (the bug) ran back and forth across his path right there by his feet. Now he became angry. He placed his basket down, and again he chased it. I do not know where it hid.

On the fifth day then he heard them laughing. So he went along even more painstakingly. Now that thing went still more back and forth in front of him by his feet. He forgot in his great irritation and tension, he loosened and let go his pack basket. "Oh oh oh" his children sounded and at once died from the shock of the sudden movement of the basket. All done, finished, and he again put back his basket on himself. When he went along now he did not hear them talking at all. He went along then. They were dead now when he uncovered his basket. Only bones were inside it. He reached his house. The following day then he buried them. He finished with that effort. He wept for five days.

Then he said, "Indeed I myself did like that and lost my children because of my own doing. The people who will populate this country are coming and close by now. Only in that one manner shall it be, when persons die. In that one way had I brought my children back, then the people would be like that.

When they died in summertime wintertime or toward springtime, after the leaves came on the trees all the dead, would have come back to life, and such persons would have revived on the fifth day following a ritual like the one I attempted. But now any mourner's sorrow departs from him after ten days of formal mourning. Then he can go to anywhere where something entertaining is happening, or they are gambling and he may shed his mourning and watch it."

CLACKAMAS (B)

Every word in this narrative contributes to its dramatically infolding structure that compels us to imagine the costs of refusing to listen – even to a troublesome child. A Clackamas audience would have **heard** *(as we cannot) sounds of the words, and so more directly felt the silencing that creates a dark configuration of threats and fears within the intimacies of family life. Our common humanity allows us to understand difficulties posed by a new wife or a child's impolitic curiosity. But we are unfamiliar with the normal life in a well-built but small house that is without separate bedrooms or bathrooms, and with light only from a central fire. So lived Seal, her brother and her daughter, comfortable with each others' movements, sounds, and behavior, until the intrusion of the new "wife" – whose doubtfulness of person, gender, and of role exacerbates the readjustments in established mutual accommodations among family members.*

Seal shushing her daughter's claim that the sound of her aunt's urination is unusual manifests an etiquette of tolerance through pretended non-observation. But useful manners here appear to have facilitated murder. We must listen carefully to sounds and words (even those of children), but we must act judiciously on what we hear. It is difficult to balance respect for the privacies of the individual with interventions necessary to success of the family unit. The abruptness of the story's slightly unusual concluding formula, "Now I remember only that far," urges upon listeners an imaginative rerehearsal of the frustrations of the daughter's repeated (and repeatedly dismissed) efforts to gain a hearing about what she's heard. These repetitions would increase in power as every retelling of the story (probably in the dimness of a firelit interior) deepened rather than dispelled the mystery beneath its sensationalism. But we **readers***, less familiar with hearing urination in earth, and attentive more to semantics than*

Figure 2 Northwest Indian house. This posed picture illustrates a Chilikat house, its decorations and carvings, as well as traditional costumes and artifacts, all characteristic of Northwest Coast Indian styles of sculpture, dress, and ornamentation that might have been found in the Clackamas home of Seal, her brother, and daughter in story 17. Specially relevant to that story are the beautifully carved doorposts seen here, the figures on which always represent family history and lineages. These carvings suggest how complexly meaningful for the story's native audience were the implications in Seal's terse comment in story 17 that the doorposts of her brother's house are "valuable." ("Chilikat Carvings in Koh-Klux's Big House," Pratt Collection 567, NA 3073, reproduced by permission of the Digital Collections of the University of Washington.)

word sounds (onomatopoeia is used in the original), are likely to overlook the fearful social responsibilities of listening and interpreting dramatized in this dialogic narrative. Our insoluble problems (for example, how to assess the reference to valuable doorposts? – meaning the brother was a wealthy man and therefore a "good" one? a revelation of Seal's extreme value for prestige and family tradition?) raise the possibility that for its original Indian hearers the story's most disturbing quality may have been its offering so little critical distance. The storytellers' imaginative enactment **performs** *fundamental tensions in the Clackamas code of behavior; what may have gripped original listeners was that, although taught to listen very carefully, they were left wondering how best to evaluate these narrated events.*

17

From Melville Jacobs, "Seal and Her Younger Brother Lived There," *International Journal of American Linguistics* 25:2 (1959), 340–1. Quoted with permission of the University of Chicago Press.

They lived there, Seal, her daughter, and Seal's younger brother. I do not know when it was, but now a woman got to Seal's younger brother and remained as his wife. They lived there.

They all would go outside at night in order to urinate. The girl would speak, she would tell her mother, "Mother! There is something different about my uncle's wife. She is just like a man when she goes out." "Do not speak like that! She is your uncle's wife!" They lived there like that for a long long time. They went outside in the nighttime. And then she would say to her, "Mother! There is something different about my uncle's wife. When she goes outside it sounds just like a man." "Do not talk like that!"

Her uncle and his wife would lie together in bed. Some time afterwards the two of them lay close to the fire, they lay close beside it. I do not know what time of night it was, something dripped on her face. She shook her mother. She said to her, "Mother! Something dripped on my face." "Hm. Do not say that. Your uncle and his wife are copulating." Presently then she again heard something dripping down. She said to her, "Mother! I hear something dripping." "Oh don't now. Your uncle and his wife are copulating." The girl got up, she fixed the fire, she lit pitch, she looked where they were lying in bed. Oh! Oh! Blood! She raised her light to it. In the bed her uncle's neck was severed. He was dead. She screamed.

She said to her mother, "I told you something was dripping. You said to me, Oh don't say that. They are copulating. I told you there was something different about my uncle's wife. When she went outside she urinated exactly like a man. You said to me, Don't say that!" She wept. Seal said, "Younger brother! My younger brother! The house posts in my younger brother's house are valuable standing there. My younger brother!" She kept saying that.

But the girl herself wept. She said, "I tried to tell you but in vain, My uncle's wife urinated not like a woman but just like a man. You said to me, Don't say that! Oh oh my uncle! Oh my uncle!" The girl wept.

Now I remember only that far.

HOPI

This tale's expansive repetitions contrast illuminatingly with the self-enclosing repeti-tiveness of the preceding Clackamas story. Here, as in the following Wintu narrative, contrast/parallelism structure is replaced by a sequential form more familiar to us, because the deepest source of tension lies in the increasing inevitability of the defeat of the Hopi boy and the powers supporting him. For the Hopi audience the important revelation is not of the girl's identity but of the dangerous dynamics of an environment whose balance is maintained only by a ruthless competition of diverse natural potencies – epitomized by the dark linkage of sex and survival to violent death.

We think of hide-and-seek as a child's game, but a Hopi audience would immediately recognize the stakes in this story are life and death even before the girl proposes the deadly prize, because the narrative instantly conjoins the Hopi's two principal food sources, agriculture and hunting. The boy, sent to guard crops against birds and animals, is seduced by the girl (whose food he unwisely eats) into a competition in which her skill as huntress dominates him. Through adroit use of her body she defeats him both in concealment and discovery, even though he not only cheats but is also helped by the powerful mythological figure of Spider Woman and the Sun – vital to the growth of crops. The girl depends entirely on herself. Her strength lies in her mastery of the individual skills needed for successful hunting, which demands quick responses to unpredictable situations and a gift for improvising strategies. Systematic planning and cooperativeness are more essential to communal farming – perhaps why the story so ingeniously evokes association between predators' success and sexual maneuvering.

The tiny, short-lived fly, who competes with humans for dead meat, engineers the boy's resurrection and the girl's expulsion from inside Hopi culture – at the cost of making hunting forever difficult. Now to find game men must make

Figure 3 Hopi pottery. These examples of Hopi pottery were gathered together to illustrate the distinctive artistry of form and design that clearly distinguishes them from any other Native American pottery, even that made by closely related Pueblo peoples. This uniqueness of visual artistic style undoubtedly has its equivalents in the storytelling of different Indian peoples, but we have not yet adequately identified the literary characteristics that distinguish Hopi stories, such as 18, even from that of peoples with a very different history in a distant part of the continent, such as the Seneca – see stories 9 and 10.

("Collection of Moquii Ware," X-30242, reproduced by permission of the Denver Public Library.)

offerings in the dark to the bloody female spirit. Thus the narrative manipulates conventionalized gender roles to articulate how the human community is tensely entangled with every other element of the natural world, reminding listeners of the terribly simple truth that the game of culture depends on the death of others – to the benefit also of flies.

18
From H. R. Voth, *The Traditions of the Hopi*. Chicago: Publications of Field Columbian Museum 8 (1905), 16–21.

In Oraibi the people were living. At the west end of the south row of houses lived a youth. A short distance north-east of the present Honáni kiva lived a maiden. One day the youth went down to the west side of the mesa to watch his father's fields. As he passed the house of the maiden she asked where he was going. "I am going to watch my father's fields," he said. "May I not go along?" she asked. "Yes," he said, thinking that she was only joking, and passed on. She wrapped up some fresh píki rolls and followed the youth. "So you have come," he said to her by way of greeting when she had arrived. "Yes," she said, and opening her blanket showed him her píki, which they ate together. "Let us play hide and seek now," she said, "and the one who is found four times shall be killed." "All right," he replied, "you hide first because you wanted it." "No, you hide first," she said, and so finally they agreed that the girl would go and hide first. "But you must not look after me," she warned the youth, and spread her blanket (ushímni) over him.

She then ran through the growing corn and finally hid under some corn-stalks. As soon as she had hidden she called out "tow." The young man then commenced to hunt her but could not find her. Finally he said: "I cannot find you, come out." So she came out and they went back to the place where they had eaten, and the youth then went to hide himself, covering up the girl with her blanket. He hid under a saltbush. Having hidden, he called out, "tow," whereupon the girl hunted for him and found him. Hereupon they again returned, the youth was covered up and the girl again went among the growing corn to hide. Finding a large corn-stalk, she pulled out the tassel, crawled into the opening and put the tassel in again. She then signaled to the youth, and he came and looked for her. Following her tracks he found that she had been running through the corn-field. So he hunted throughout the corn-field and then at the edge among the herbs and grasses, but could not find her. Finally he noticed that her tracks seemed to come to an end near a large corn-stalk, but he could not find her anywhere. Finally he called out, "I cannot find you, where are you?" "Here I am," she replied, and throwing out the corn-tassel she jumped out. So for the second time he had failed to find her.

They again returned to the edge of the field, the girl now covering herself up. The youth now, as he went through the field, was thinking, "Where shall I hide? It is time that she does not find me again." As he passed along the edge of the field he heard a voice. "Listen to me," some one said. "Come up here. I have pity on you. One time she has already found you, and she will certainly find you again." This was the Sun. Hereupon the latter threw down a rainbow upon which the youth climbed to the Sun, who hid him behind his back saying, "Here she will not find you." So the girl followed his tracks all through the field, and went to the edge of the field to a small knoll, but could not find him. She followed them again throughout the field and returned to the same place. By this time she was puzzled where he could be. Her hair whorls were hanging down out of shape. She was thinking and thinking where he might be. Finally she pressed a few drops of milk out of her breast, examined the drops in her hand, and seeing the sun reflected in them, she discovered the boy behind him. She at once said, "Aha, there you are; I have found you. Come down."

The youth now again covered himself up and the girl went to hide away the third time. But this time the youth lifted up a corner of the covering and watched her, in which direction she went. When he followed her tracks throughout the corn-field he could not find her. Her tracks led to a patch of watermelons and squashes, but as the runners covered the ground he could not find her there. He returned to the corn-field and hunted, but not finding her anywhere he again followed her tracks to the watermelon patch. Finally he gave up in despair and called out, "I cannot find you, come out." She then burst open a watermelon, saying, "Here I am, and you did not find me," and came out.

The youth by this time became unhappy. They again returned and the maiden covering herself up, the youth went to hide away, but was very unhappy. Running through the corn-field and along its edge, he all at once heard a voice. "Where are you going? I have pity on you. You come in here," and looking down he saw a small hole by the side of a small corn-stalk. It was the house of Spider Woman. This he entered and she quickly spun some web across the opening. The girl again went to hunt for the youth. Running through the corn-field repeatedly, she finally traced his tracks to the edge of the corn-field, but could not find him anywhere. She then drew forth from her bosom a mirror made from a quartz crystal. Through this she hunted first upward, hoping to find him somewhere above again, but failed to find him. She then turned it downward and all at once saw the opening of the Spider's hole reflected in it. "Come out," she at once called out, "I have found you. You are in there." Spider Woman said, "Well, you will have to go out, she has found you." He was very dejected by this time because there was only one chance for him left; but he came out.

For the fourth time the girl went to hide away. The youth again lifted up a corner of the covering and looked after her and saw that she was again running towards the watermelon patch. On one side of the corn-field was a ditch and as it had rained shortly before, there was some water in this ditch and a number of tadpoles were in this water. The girl crossed the watermelon patch, went into the ditch, entered the water and turned into a tadpole. The boy again went in search of the girl, following her tracks through the corn-field and through the watermelon patch down to the ditch, but failed to find her. He returned and hunted throughout the field, and being very tired, he returned to the water, stooped down and drank some. He was very sad by this time, but he hunted once more. Finally he again followed her tracks to the edge of the water, and knowing that she must be there somewhere, he called out, "I cannot find you, just come out," and immediately she emerged from the water and said, "I was here when you were drinking water and I looked right at you." He then remembered that a tadpole had looked up out of the water when he was drinking, but he, of course, never thought that that could be the maiden.

So they returned again to the same place, and as they went back the youth was very much discouraged. "Only one chance left for me," he thought, "where shall I hide that she will not find me?" After the girl had covered herself he again went away. Passing the house of Spider Woman, the latter said to him, "Alas! where are you going? You go there a little to the east to your uncle, the Áhū (a species of worm that lives in rotten wood); he lives in the takáchi (a temporary shelter) and maybe he will hide you." So the youth went there and when he arrived there called out, "My uncle, put me in there." So the Áhū pulled out a loose knot from one of the corner poles, which was that of a piñon-tree. This post was hollow, and into this the Áhū put the youth, closing up the opening after he had entered. So the girl went and hunted for the youth, following his tracks through the corn-field, and found that he had been going up and down and back and forth, and finally she tracked them to the shelter. Arriving at this place she hunted, but at first could not find him. She then put the tips of her right-hand fingers, one after another, into her mouth, wet them slightly, then pressed the point of her forefinger into her right ear, and immediately she heard the youth in his hiding place and told him to come out, as she had found him.

They then returned to their place again, but the girl said: "Let us now return again to the shelter where I found you." So they returned and sat down close to the shelter on the north side. The girl hereupon dug a hole close to one of the corner posts and then said to the youth: "I have beaten you, I have beaten you. You take off your shirt." He did so. It was a blue shirt such as the Hopi used to wear. "Now take off your beads," she said, and, not knowing what she intended to do, he did so. She hereupon grabbed him by the hair, jerked out a knife from behind her belt, bent him over the hole that she had made, and cut his throat, letting the blood run into the hole. She then closed up this hole, dug another one somewhat to the north and dragged the body to it, burying it in this grave.

Hereupon she took the shirt and the beads with her and went home. When the young man did not return to his home his parents became worried and inquired at the maiden's house. "We thought you both had gone to our field to watch," they said. "Do you not know where Kwavúhü is?" "Yes," she said, "we were there together, but he drove me away, and I do not know where he is." So the parents were very sad. They had killed a sheep shortly before, but as they were so sorry they ate very little of the meat, and so the flies came in and ate of the meat. One time the woman was driving the flies off with a broom and one of them said, "Why do you drive me away when I eat your meat? I suck some of this meat and then I shall go and hunt your child." Hereupon the woman desisted and the flies then sucked of the meat. "Yes," the woman then said to the fly, "our boy went to watch the fields and he never came back. If you can, you go and hunt him and find him for me." So the Fly flew away to the corn-field and found very many tracks. Following them all over the field, she finally tracked them to the shelter where the young man had been killed. Flying around here she soon discovered traces of the blood, and opening the hole she found blood in it. She sucked some of this blood out and went a little farther north and there found the grave. She then sucked up all the blood from the first opening and injected it into the body and then waited. Soon the heart of the youth began to beat and after a little while he raised up, shaking his head slightly. "Have you woken up?" the Fly said. "Yes," he answered, "but I am very thirsty." "There is some water over there in the ditch," the Fly said, "go there and drink and then we shall return to your house." So then he went there and quenched his thirst and then they returned to the house of his parents. These were now very happy when they saw the child. The Fly then said to the parents, "The shirt and beads of your boy are at the maiden's house. Let him go over there and then see what she says, whether she will be glad or not, and then let him ask for his shirt and beads, and when she gives him the shirt let him shake it at her, and then when he gets the beads he must shake them, too."

The mother then said to her son, "All right, you go over to the house." But the Fly continued, "She will probably spread food before you, she will offer you piki rolls, but do not eat them." So he went over there. When the girl saw him she exclaimed, "Ih (with a rising inflection), have you come?" "Yes," he said, "I have come." "Sit down," she said to him, and at once went into another room and got some food, which she placed before him. "I am not hungry; I have come for my shirt and my beads. I think you brought them with you when you came." "Yes, I have them here, and of course I shall give them to you." She hereupon went into a room and when she opened the door the young man looked in and saw that she was very wealthy. She had a great many things there that she had taken from the youths whom she had killed. When she brought out his things, he took them and shook them at her and said, "Yes, these are mine, these are the ones." Hereupon he left the house, but the Fly had in the meanwhile told his parents that they should go over to the girl's house also and meet their son there, so they met in front of the house and waited there. While they were standing there they heard a noise in the house, some clapping and shaking. When the young man had shaken his shirt and the beads at the girl, an evil charm had entered her and she was changed into "Tihkuy Wuhti" (child protruding woman). She entered an inner room and came out dressed in a white robe. Her hair was now tied up like that of a married woman, but her face and clothes were all bloody. While she had put on this costume the noise and rattle in the room where the costumes of the slain youths were had continued, and these costumes, which it seems consisted mostly of buckskins, rabbit skins, etc., had assumed the shape of deer, antelope, and rabbits, and these now dashed out of the room and left the house. The girl tried to keep them and was angry, but could not stop them. She grabbed the last one, however, and wiping her hand over her genitalia she rubbed this hand over the face of the antelope, twisted his nose, rubbed his horns, etc., and then let him run. She then turned to the people who had assembled outside of the house and said, "After this you shall have great difficulty in hunting these animals. If you had let them alone here, they would have remained close by, and you would have had no difficulty in slaying them." She thereupon also left the house and disappeared with the game. Ever after she lived along the Little Colorado River, where also for a long time the deer and antelope abounded. And this is the reason why it is so difficult to approach and kill this game. The Tíhkuy Wuhti having rubbed her own odor over the nose and face of that antelope, these antelopes now smell the odor of people from a far distance, and so it is very difficult to approach them. The Tíhkuy Wuhti is said to still live at the Little Colorado River, and the Hopi claim to have seen her, still wrapped up in the white robe, and all covered with blood. She controls the game, and hunters make prayer-offerings to her of turquoise and nakwákwosis stained in red ochre like that used in the Snake ceremony. These prayer-offerings, however, are always deposited in the night.

WINTU

Indians frequently chose a sequential form of storytelling (the kind we know best) when the purpose of the story was to challenge an important social regulation – in this case, an incest taboo. The cause–effect mode is helpful for plain definition of the necessity for the prohibition, but at the same time can effectively dramatize the naturalness of the impulse that provoked establishment of the interdiction – as well as its possible monstrous consequences. The point of this story (like others of its kind) is neither to encourage incest nor to insist dogmatically on the necessity of the prohibition. The story creates imaginative space within which teller and audience together explore the basis and effects of a significant social institution. The storytelling nurtures understanding of a system of communal control in a complicated world of competing energies that allow no absolute or simple solutions. That understanding, I would argue, is perhaps the highest achievement of human consciousness.

This narrative begins with a girl breaking rules of Wintu gender relations by "bothering" the family's prized son. Her playful roughhousing threatens to arouse him sexually. Her older sister, having internalized Wintu conventions of proper gender roles, insists the girl (who thinks the wrestling is innocent, not "bothering") restrain and conceal her blossoming sexuality. Traditional control here works all too efficiently. Instead of merely hiding her body, the girl, going beyond the adolescent anorexia familiar to us, literally makes her body disappear. She consumes herself, and her corrupted appetite endangers her entire family, finally engulfing the too-cherished brother. The story enforces awareness of the "healthy" naturalness of impulses toward incest which social artifices must suppress or reorient. That, as Freud spent his life insisting, can produce monsters, self-dehumanized people.

The story ends with loss for both individual and society. The girl, in the guise of a loon with its weirdly haunting cry and its "necklace" of heart-shaped markings, is killed by her younger brother, but the older brother's resurrection fails. There is no easy solution to the problems of channeling natural impulses into productive familial/social institutions. As is true of a majority of Native American stories, the central purpose of this deliberately troubling tale is cautionary but not coercive.

19

From Cora Du Bois and Dorothy Demetracopoulou, *Wintu Myths*. Berkeley: University of California Publications in American Archaeology and Ethnology, 28:5 (1921), 360–2.

Long ago, there came into being some people who had four children, two boys and two girls, and who owned a big earth lodge. The adolescent boy stayed in the earth lodge always. In the meantime his younger sister reached adolescence. So they left her in the menstrual hut for some nights. Now his younger sister loved him who was in the earth lodge. So she went to him, got into bed with him, tickled him and sat all over him. However her elder brother said, "What is the matter with you, younger sister?" and she left. So she came to him, sometimes in the evening, sometimes in the early morning, and she bothered him as before, tickling him. And as before he said, "What is the matter with you, younger sister?" So at last her elder brother told his sister. "Elder sister, here to me, all the time to me, comes to me my younger sister," he said. And his sister went to her younger sister and asked, "Why do you always bother my younger brother?" And the other said, "I never bother him." Then the other said, "Younger sister, go get maple. Make yourself a front apron." So she went to get it, climbed around on the maple trees and peeled, kept on peeling, and cut her finger. And for a while she stood there with blood dripping to the ground. Then she sucked the blood. She did not know what to do, so she sucked it in and spat it out, and as she did so the blood tasted sweet to her, so now, first because she wanted to swallow blood and then because she wanted to eat her flesh, she devoured her flesh and turned into a Rolling Head. All around the world she went, devouring people. She left for herself only her elder sister, her younger brother, and her elder brother.

Now they were afraid and started to climb up above. They heard her below going about wildly everywhere asking everything, the rock beings, the tree beings, asking all. And they said, "We don't know." They added, "You grew into something else and yet you know nothing." So she asked some ancient faeces and they said, "You grew into something else and yet you know nothing. Look up above." So she looked up and saw them going halfway up. So she jumped up, and grabbed, and pulled down, and then lay on her back, and spread her legs. He who was going above, her elder brother, fell between her thighs. She was very excited.

And the rest went above empty-handed. "Oh dear, our own child has orphaned us," said the old man. They cried. And the older daughter said, "However long it may take, I'll find my younger brother." So they went up above.

Now her older brother would have nothing to do with her, and turned on his side. So, in one lick as it were, she devoured him, his heart alone she hung around her neck and went toward the north drainage, alighted with it on a big lake, swam about with it, stayed there with it. Every evening at sunset she came, skimming the water, to a large sandy beach on the east shore, south, south to the sandy beach, on the south she alighted and stayed.

The people wanted to catch her but did not know how. Humming-Bird said, "Let me go," he said, "Let me watch." The people said, "Yes," and he said to the elder sister, "Make a good cooking basket," he said. "Then have on hand white rocks, good ones which will hold heat," he said. He did not come, and did not come, and then finally he arrived. He arrived and told them, "I saw her," he said, "She has a heart hung around her neck. At sunset she alights on the sand on the south beach. From the north she comes." And the people said, "Let's go and watch," they said. Then they said to the little boy, "You go and watch," they said. They gave him a good sharp untipped arrow. "When you see her, pierce her, and when you pierce her she'll go south, she'll get out and make a bee-line, and go south to the sand beach." To the woman they said, "You go and sit on the south bank, on the sandy beach. Have the cooking basket half full of water and heat the white rocks well and drop them in. And when he pierces her go quickly, get her, grab her, and slip the heart off over her head. Put it into the cooking basket and cover it up quickly."

At sunset they were there. And the elder sister sat on the south bank on the beach, as she had already been directed. She went there and watched. As she watched at sunset the water was heard roaring in the north. She did not come, and then, at last, she saw her come and get out on the south bank, and behold, she had been pierced by the untipped arrow. She went quickly and slipped off the heart and put it into the cooking basket. Then she took it home. "This is my younger brother's heart," she said. So they steamed it, and while they were steaming it, it came to life, but though he was a person he did not look right. He did not live very long.

YANA

This story, in conjunction with the three preceding it, offers a sample of the variety of narrative forms Native Americans employed in their storytelling. But just as the cave paintings of Chauvet and Lascaux tantalize us with unverifiable possibilities of meaning through their elegantly stylized representations of extinct animals, so Native American stories again and again tantalize us with the brilliance of their narrative form – whose meaningfulness to original tellers and audiences continues to elude us. This tale consists almost entirely of dialog, with the speakers identified only by implicit references within their speech. Yana audiences, of course, would have been familiar with the story and so would have rapidly recognized the identity of each speaker, even if the storyteller did not give each personage a characterizing vocal style. But the story seems shaped to force even a native audience momentarily to pause and think, "Ah, now the husband laments," or "Yes, the mother is remembering the daughter's words." This device of rhetorical hesitancy (a kind of inversion of repetition) seems peculiarly appropriate to the story's subtle exploration of a mysterious death, with its uncertainty intensified by the profound grief it evokes in which communal and private feelings intertwine. The narrative opens with a young man taking the initiative and giving orders to others in a manner that proves they are engaged in a communal enterprise. The speaker leads, but also listens and asks for agreement. In his absence his wife drowns in acting against the recommendations of the group, and perhaps his earlier warnings. Her death evokes recriminations and self-recriminations in both the group and her husband, and finally her mother, who then recalls her daughter's telling of her dream of dying. This retrospective movement from social present to personal past brings no certitude, except that, because the tribe is composed of distinct individuals, the most private of experiences are crucial to the tribal community. Following this story with difficulty, we may

Figure 4 Yana fishing. "Ishi," a Yahi/Yana of northern California, with his fishing harpoon, near a stream perhaps like that in which the young wife in the Yana story 20 drowned. As a young boy Ishi was one of a small group of Yahi who went into hiding in 1870 when the rest of his tribe was brutally exterminated by white Californians. When, in 1911, he became the lone survivor of this group that had lived unknown to whites for four decades, he emerged from hiding and found a home in the Hearst Museum in San Francisco until his death in 1916. This photograph was taken in 1914 while Ishi was revisiting, with white friends, the places where for so long he had lived in concealment, totally apart from white civilization.

("Ishi with Harpoon," 15-5739, reproduced by permission of the Phoebe Apperson Hearst Museum of Anthropology and the Regents of the University of California.)

dimly perceive how, in an oral culture, carefully structured storytelling articulates the social meanings of wilful behavior, intensely subjective psychological experiences, and personal struggles with overwhelming guilt and grief following violent death. Death alone is definitive, a life's limit, but the human group stays alive by repeatedly confronting that limit imaginatively, through telling and retelling stories that endow the mysteries in every human heart with more than personal significance.

20

From Edward Sapir, *Yana Texts*. Berkeley: University of California Publications in American Archaeology and Ethnology 9 (1910), 140–2.

"Now dig for roots. The nuts are already ripe – let's climb the sugar pines. We'll move down there tomorrow and get settled. Now I am going to climb for the sugar-pine nuts, they are already ripe. The other people will all come down there where there's a nice spring and we'll settle in. I think the others will come here first. We'll wait for them."

A great many people gathered there. "Now let's climb for sugar-pine nuts, and take food with us. You women dig for tiger-lilies, get winter food for yourselves. You probably don't want to climb. If you finish here, there will be winter food for everybody."

   *   *   *   *   *   *   *

"I could swim in the water over there. Let me see, let's go to drink."

"Don't go to drink."

"Why should I be afraid? I'm going to drink." She saw logs bobbing up and down in the water. "Let me see. I can swim over there to the west."

They looked around for her but didn't see her.

"Let me see. I'll try it. I can swim across there."

"You won't be able to swim across the water."

She took off her skirt. "I'm going in to swim. Just watch me!"

She swam westward. Many of them saw her. Now she sank between the logs.

"We told you of that danger."

Her buckskin skirt and tassels beaded with pine nuts lay there as she had left them. Then they cried.

   *   *   *   *   *   *   *

"Why are you crying?"

"She is drowning."

"I told you , 'Keep her away from the water!' It is your fault. I should have been here myself. I can't believe I came here for this! What can I do? Let us search for her! Please let's see if we can find her. Let's try something. She is a good woman. You, run back to the other people – they should come here."

The man ran back, telling the others to come. "Yes," they answered.

"Let me see, go ahead. I'll try something."

They try to divert the water by means of a ditch.

"We probably won't be able to draw off the water, it won't be diverted."

"Then what should we do? All of you clean out that ditch. I don't think we will find her. I know we won't find her. She must have sunk straight down, sunk down there between the two logs. That's a bad place."

    *   *   *   *   *   *

They all went back home, most dispersing. Some stayed together.

"No longer will I collect winter food . Now I've done with that. Alas, I was happy. I didn't think this would happen to me. I shall live no longer."

"Why, tell me, did you let her go off? You should have taken water with you. You were foolish."

"I didn't know. I should have gone with her, but she just ran off by herself. She should have told me, 'Let's go and drink.' She was angry. I am no good. My heart is torn."

They all arrived home and lay down in the ashes of the fireplace, even the men. Her people who had climbed for the sugar-pine nuts cried; they threw the pine-nuts into the fire.

    *   *   *   *   *   *

Long before she had said: "Perhaps I shall never again enter this house. I dreamt that I was dying. Please, burn up all of these things."

"Daughter, I'm fearful when you speak that way."

"We'll probably be away two months climbing for sugar-pine nuts, and I may die. Perhaps I shall not again enter my home."

"I'll cry because you speak that way."

"You'll find out it is true."

    *   *   *   *   *   *

Her mother wept. Now she is dead. Her hair comes flying back home. It comes blowing back home.

"I shall surely have died if my hair comes back here, blown by the wind."

"Take your tasseled buckskin skirt along with your apron fringed with white grass. Put your beads around your neck."

"Yes," she had said. "Now, mother, you stay, I go. You will never see me again."

"I am afraid. Stay at home. I am afraid for you."

"Father, do not feel bad. Just cry a little bit for me. You'll grow old. Mother, please do not cry much. If you see people eating in the next house, do not go over. If you see food over there, just lower your eyes. You had the happiness of bringing me up. Then I did not think about taking a husband."

NAVAJO

The final narratives are selected to illustrate, albeit faintly, the penetration into Native American storytelling of the Indians' sense of belonging to the sacred processes of the natural world. This sense is profound, permeating all the workings of their minds and bodies, ingrained into the very texture of their thought and feeling by personal experience and cultural traditions created out of long histories of similar experience. This pervasive sense of belonging makes it rare to find in their stories descriptive passages or analysis of subjective feelings about natural phenomena so common in our writing. Such descriptions and analyses in fact are evidence of our alienation from nature, and our loss of any sense for the sacredness of its vitality.

The following is a tiny excerpt from a myth that would take many, many hours to tell, one foundation for a major Navajo healing ceremony, the Mountain Chant. The young Navajo protagonist, disobeying his father's injunction not to hunt to the south, is captured by Ute Indians. He escapes them through the aid of one of the numerous **yei** *(Navajo divinities), Talking God. Intimate knowledge of and deep emotional attachment to the landscape saturates this narrative, as it does many Navajo stories. So complete and intense is the interconnection between man and land that only once is the hero's profound sensitivity for the beauty of his homeland made explicit – appropriately the moment when, disobeying his father's command, he has chosen to turn away from the place where he belongs. This occurs in the opening paragraph of the excerpt and establishes the mood of poignant homesickness for the La Plata Mountains that pervades the entire myth.*

This psychic linkage to the physical environment is the foundation of a religiosity that may disconcert readers familiar only with monotheism. The varieties of Native American polytheism are incredibly diverse, but the Navajo form is reasonably representative, especially in its refusal to distinguish natural from supernatural. For the

Navajo, all physical nature is divine – illness is a breakdown of the beautiful, healthy unity of what we call "spirit" and "body," environment and individual. Because the natural environment is never static but perpetually moving in a multitude of different ways, the divinity of existence is unfixed and complicated. The famous Navajo prayer "May I walk in beauty" epitomizes the dynamism of their religion.

*Perhaps our only way to come close to understanding Navajo polytheism is to think of it as an ecosystem. The divinity of the cosmos is constituted by multifarious forces constantly influencing each other and self-transforming – to no purpose beyond that of sustaining the vitality of the whole. This requires a continuous balancing and rebalancing of an intricate interaction of energies. Necessarily, then, a Navajo's relations to any of his some two hundred gods is always threatened by uncertainty; it demands perpetual alertness to one's ever-shifting position within an environment whose essential force is moving, invisible air, whether the blowing wind or our own breathing. There are many powers, and at any given moment the configuration of their relations to one another and to people can change. Hints of this instability appear in Talking God's behavior to the protagonist, whom he seems to enjoy teasing as much as saving. Illustrated here is the fashion in which Navajo religiosity (like that of most Native American peoples) demands a constant attentiveness to the potential multi-dimensional consequences of the **style** of one's speech and behavior, not just care during special times or ceremonies. Normal daily behavior of Native Americans compared to ours was ceremonious, because for them the spiritual inhered in every act. This Navajo myth exemplifies how Indians' alertness to every nuance of shift in their environment assisted not merely physical survival but also the attainment of spiritual well-being. For such listeners even the thrill of a hero's escape from marauding enemies is less exciting than the story's revitalization of their feeling for the extraordinary beauty, danger, and wonder of living appropriately in a familiar world always more than equal to the fullest powers of their imagination.*

21

From Washington Matthews, *The Mountain Chant: A Navajo Ceremony.* Washington, DC: Annual Report of the Bureau of American Ethnology, 5 (1883–4).

On the morrow, when he went forth on his hunt, his father gave him the usual injunctions, saying: "Hunt in any direction from the lodge that you will; but go not to the south." He departed as if he were going to the east; but when he got out of sight from the hogán he turned round to the south and pursued his way in that direction. He went on until he came to the San Juan River, and he forded it at a place a little above Beautiful Under the Cottonwoods, where they had crossed it before. He went on to a place called Erect Cat Tail Rushes and thence to a place called Clay Hill. Here he laid his deer skin mask and his weapons on the ground and climbed the hill to observe the surrounding country for game. But instead of looking south in the direction in which he was going he looked to the north, the country in which dwelt his people. Before him were the beautiful peaks of La Plata with their forested slopes. The clouds hung over the mountain, the showers of rain fell down its sides, and all the country looked beautiful. And he said to the land, "Aqalàni!" (greeting), and a feeling of loneliness and homesickness came over him, and he wept and sang this song:

> That flowing water! That flowing water!
> My mind wanders across it.
> That broad water! That flowing water!
> My mind wanders across it.
> That old age water! That flowing water!
> My mind wanders across it.

The gods heard his song and they were about to gratify his wishes. He was destined to return to La Plata but not in the manner he most desired. Had he gazed to the south when he ascended the hill, instead of to the north, it might have been otherwise.

He wiped away his tears and went down to the place where he had laid his mask and arms at the foot of the hill. He put on his buckskin coat and was just putting on his mask, but had not quite drawn it down over his head, when he heard a noise to the south and, looking around, he saw a great crowd on horseback riding towards him. To see better he drew off his mask, and then observed that they were dividing into two lines as they advanced; a moment later he was surrounded. The horsemen were of the tribe of Ute, a people whose language he did not understand. One young man rode up close to the Navajo, aimed an arrow at the breast of the latter and drew it to the head; but just as he was about to release it an old man began to address the party in a loud voice and the young warrior lowered his arrow and relaxed his bow. Then the speaker dismounted, approached the captive, and seized him by the arm. For a long time there was much loud talking and discussion among the Ute. Now one would harangue the party and then another would make a speech, but after a while the dispute ceased and the old man motioned to the Navajo to move on. They made him trot while they followed him on horseback in a semicircle, so that they could guard him and watch his movements. Soon they came to Deep Sands; shortly afterward they crossed the San Juan. That night they camped near a spring, where they watched him closely all night and gave him nothing to eat. They bound his feet firmly together, tied his hands behind his back, and threw an untanned buckskin over him before they lay down to sleep.

They set out on their journey again early in the morning. At Scattered Springs they stopped for a little while to eat, but the only food they gave the Navajo was the full of his palm of service berries. When they arrived on the south side of Narrow Water they halted for the night and a number went out to hunt. Among them they secured two deer, one large and one small; the feet of these they gave to their captive for his supper. Next morning they gave him a piece of liver, half of which he ate and the rest he kept. They moved on rapidly and rested for the night where there was a spring. They had given him nothing to eat all that day, and at night they gave him nothing; so it was well for him that he had secreted part of the liver. This he ate after dark. On the third morning he had to set out fasting and had to go on foot as usual. About noon, however, one of the Ute took pity on him and lent him a horse to ride, while the owner of the horse walked all the afternoon. That night they arrived at the bank of a large river, and here they gave him to understand, by signs, that this was the last river they would cross until they got home. Beyond the river there was nothing in sight but a great plain.

By the light of the morning, however, on the next day, he discerned some mountains showing their points faintly above the northern horizon. To these the Ute pointed and motioned to him to go ahead. They did not follow him immediately; but saddled up at their leisure while the Navajo went on. Though he was now for some time alone on the trail and out of sight of his captors, he knew that he could not escape; all around and before him was a desert plain where he could not discover a single hiding place; so he trudged on, tired and hungry and sorrowing, and he wept all along the way. At noon they gave him another handful of berries.

At night they came to a plain situated between four mountains, one on the east, one on the south, one on the west, and one on the north, and here there was a great encampment of Ute, whose tents were scattered around in different places on the plain. There was one tent whose top was painted black and whose base was painted white and which had a forked pole set in the ground in front of it. To this his master, the old man who had saved his life and taken him by the arm on the occasion of his capture, led him, while the rest of the war party departed to their respective tents. The old man hung his own arms and acconterments on the pole, and the slave, following his example, hung his deer skin mask and robe on the forks and laid his crutches against the pole, and he prayed to the head of the deer, saying:

> Whenever I have appealed to you, you have helped me, my pet.
> Once you were alive, my pet.
> Take care that I do not die, my pet.
> Watch over me.

When he had finished his prayer an old man came and danced around him, and when the latter had done an old woman approached with a whistle in her hand and she whistled all around him. This was for joy because they had captured one of an alien tribe. Then his master motioned to him to go into the tent. Here he was given a large bowl of berries of which he ate his fill, and he was allowed to lie down and sleep undisturbed until morning.

Next morning the Ute began to enter the tent. They came one by one and in small groups until after a while there was a considerable crowd present. Then they gave the Navajo to understand by signs that they wished to know for what purpose he wore the mask and the buckskin. He answered that he used them for no particular purpose, but only for a whim. They repeated the question three times very pointedly and searchingly, but he continued to make evasive replies. The fourth time they addressed him they charged him to tell the truth and speak quickly, reminding him that he was a prisoner whose life was in the hands of his captors and telling him that if he did not disclose the use of his mask and robe he would be killed before sunset, while if he revealed the secret his life would be spared. He pondered but a short time over their words and determined to tell them the truth. So he explained to them the use of the mask and the robe in deceiving the deer and told the wonderful power he had of getting game by shooting into certain bushes. At dark they sent in two young men to be initiated into his mysteries. He began by giving them a full account of all his father had done and all he had shown him; he then taught them how to build the sweat-house, how to make the mask, how to shoot the pluck, and how to walk like a deer, and he made them practice the walk and the motions of the animal. All this occupied eleven days.

On the twelfth day the Ute went out to hunt, leaving few men in camp. There was a small inclosure of brushwood close to the tent; in it were two high poles on which skins were dressed. His master left him, that day, two skins to prepare, and he set to work at them and labored hard scraping and rubbing them until about noon, when he felt hungry and went into the tent to see if he could find anything to eat. He opened a bag and found it to contain dried meat; he put some of this on the coals and sat down to wait till it was done. As he watched the meat cooking he heard a noise at the deer skin door of the tent and, looking up, he beheld an old woman crawling in on her hands and knees. She passed once around the fire and went out at the door again, but before she disappeared she turned her head and addressed him, saying: "My grandchild, do something for yourself." He paused a moment in wonder at the strange vision he had seen and the strange words he had heard, and then he rushed out of the tent to follow his visitor and see who she might be. He went around the tent four times; he gazed in every direction; but no one was to be seen. During the rest of the day he worked but little. Occasionally he took up a stone and rubbed the hides; but most of the time he walked and loitered around, busy with his thoughts.

After sunrise the hunters returned with an abundance of meat. They came to the great lodge where the master of the Navajo dwelt; they extended its circumference by removing the pegs at the bottom; they stored the goods of the owner away at the outer edge, so as to leave a clear space in the center, and made everything ready for the reception of a large number of guests. After dark a great number gathered in the tent and the captive was ordered by his master to bring some water. He took two wicker bottles to a neighboring spring, filled them, and laid them on the ground beside the spring, while he went to gather some plants to stick into the months of the bottles as stoppers. As he went he heard a voice saying "Hist!" and looking in the direction whence it came he saw a form sitting in the water; it wore a mask like the head of a great owl and it was smoking a pipe. When he turned towards it, it said, "You walk around like one without sense or knowledge. Why don't you do something for yourself? When next you hear my voice it will be well for you if you walk towards it."

The voice ceased and the form of the owl man vanished. Then the Navajo put the stoppers into the vessels and carried them back. When he returned he observed that two large dogs were tied to the door, one on each side, and that three doors had been added to the lodge during his absence, so that now there were four doors covering the doorway. When he entered he found the lodge filled with Ute and he saw four bags of tobacco and four pipes lying near the fire, one at each cardinal point of the compass. He observed a very old man and a very old woman seated at the door, one on each side. A cord tied to the old woman passed round the edge of the lodge on one side, behind the spectators, to the west, and another cord, tied to the man, passed round on the opposite side of the lodge. His master bade him sit down in the west, and when he was seated one of the cords was tied to his wrists and one to his ankles, and thus he was secured to the old pair.

Now he feared more than ever for his safety; he felt sure that his captors contemplated his death by torture. The pipes were lit and the council began. The talking in the strange tongue that he could not understand had lasted long into the night, when he fancied that he heard the voice of the Yèbiteai (Talking God) above the din of human voices, saying "hu'hu'hu'hu" in the far distance. He strained his attention and listened well, and after a while he felt certain that he heard the voice again nearer and louder. It was not long until the cry was repeated for the third time, and soon after the captive heard it once more, loudly and distinctly, immediately to the west of the lodge. Then there was a sound as of footsteps at the door, and the white lightning entered through the smoke hole and circled around the lodge, hanging over the heads of the council. But the Ute heard not the voice which the Navajo heard and saw not the vision he beheld. Soon the Yaybieby (Talking God) entered the lodge and standing on the white lightning, said: "What is the matter with you, my grandchild? You take no thought about anything. Something you must do for yourself, or else, in the morning you will be whipped to death – that is what the council has decided. Pull out four pegs from the bottom of the tent, push it open there, and then you can shove things through." The Navajo answered, "How shall I do it? See the way I am tied! I am poor! See how I am wound up!" But (Talking God) again said: "When you leave, take with you those bags filled with embroideries and take with you tobacco from the pouches near the fire." Scarcely had Talking God disappeared when the Navajo heard a voice overhead, and a whippoor will flew down through the smoke hole, hovered four times around the lodge over the heads of the Ute, and departed by the way it had entered. In a moment after it had disappeared a few of the Ute began to nod and close their eyes; soon the others showed signs of drowsiness; some stretched themselves out on the ground overpowered with sleep; others rose and departed from time to time, singly and in little groups, to seek their lodges and repose there. The last to drop asleep were the old man and the old woman who sat at the door; but at length their chins fell upon their bosoms. Then the Navajo, fearing no watchers, went to work and loosened the cords that bound him; he lifted, from the inside, some of the pegs which held the edge of the tent, and shoved out the two bags of embroideries which Talking God told him to take. Passing out through the door of the lodge, where he found both the watch dogs sound asleep, and taking with him the cords with which he had been tied and some of the tobacco, he went round to the back of the lodge, where he had put the bags; these he tied with the cords in such a manner that they would make an easily balanced double bundle. He shouldered his bundle and was all ready to start.

At this moment he heard, at a little distance to the south of where he stood, the hoot of an owl. Instantly recollecting the words of the owl like form which he had encountered at the spring at nightfall, he set off in the direction from which the call proceeded. He had not walked far until he came to a precipitons bluff formed by two branching cañons, and it seemed at first impossible for him to proceed farther. Soon, however, he noticed a tall spruce tree, which grew beside the precipice from the foot to the summit, for the day had now begun to dawn and he could see objects more clearly. At this juncture Talking God again appeared to him and said: "How is it, my grandchild, that you are still here? Get on the top of that spruce tree and go down into the cañon on it." The Navajo stretched out his hand to seize the top of the tree, but it swayed away from his grasp. "See, my grandfather," he said to Talking God "it moves away from me; I cannot reach it." Then Talking God flung the white lightning around the top of the tree, as an Indian flings his lasso around the neck of a horse, and drew it in to the edge of the cliff. "Descend," he commanded the Indian, "and when you reach the bottom take four sprays from the tree, each from a different part. You may need them in the future." So the Navajo went down, took the four sprays as he was bidden and put them under his robe.

At the base of the bluff he again met Talking God and at this moment he heard a noise, as of a great and distant tumult, which seemed to come from above and from beyond the edge of the cliff whence they had descended. From moment to moment it grew louder and came nearer, and soon the sounds of angry voices could be distinguished. The Ute had discovered the flight of their captive and were in hot pursuit. "Your enemies are coming for you," said the divine one; "but yonder small holes on the opposite side of the cañon are the doors of my dwelling, where you may hide. The bottom of the cañon is strewn with large rocks and fallen trees; it would take you much time and hard labor to get over these if I did not help you; but I will do something to make your way easy." As he said this he blew a strong breath, and instantly a great white rainbow spanned the cañon. The Navajo tried to step on this in order to cross, but it was so soft that his feet went through; he could not step on it. Talking God stood beside him and laughed at his fruitless attempts to get on the rainbow. After he had enjoyed this sport sufficiently the god blew another strong breath, when at once the rainbow became as hard as ice and they both crossed it with ease. When they reached the opposite wall of the canon Talking God pointed to a very small hole in the cliff and said, "This is the door of my lodge; enter!" By this time the shouts of the Ute sounded very loud in the ears of the terrified fugitive and it seemed to him that his pursuers must have reached the edge of the opposite cliff, where they would not be long before they would see him; still, hard as he tried to enter the cave, he could not succeed; the hole was not big enough for him to put his head in. Talking God roared with laughter and slapped his hands together as he witnessed the abject fear and the fruitless efforts of the Navajo. When he had laughed enough he blew on the little hole and it spread instantly into a large orifice, through which they both entered with ease. They passed through three rooms and stopped in the fourth. Here Talking God took the bags from the back of the Navajo, opened them, and drew from them some beautifully garnished clothing – a pair of moccasins, a pair of long-fringed leggings, and a shirt. He arrayed himself in these and went out, leaving the Navajo in the cave. As soon as his rescuer was gone the fugitive heard loud noises without and the sound of many angry voices, which continued for a long, long time. At last they died away and were heard no more. The Ute had tracked him to the edge of the cliff where he got on the tree; but there they lost his trail and searched all the neighborhood to see if they could regain it; hence the noises. When all was silent Talking God returned and said, "Your enemies have departed; you can leave in safety." So, taking a tanned elk skin to cover his back and a pair of new moccasins to protect his feet, the Navajo set out from the cave.

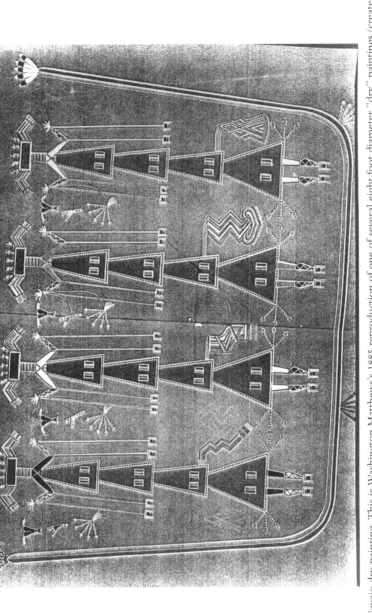

Figure 5 Navajo dry painting. This is Washington Matthews's 1885 reproduction of one of several eight-foot diameter "dry" paintings (created with sand and colored minerals) for a Mountain Chant healing ceremony, founded upon the myth of story 21. During the ceremony the patient literally walks into the painting, chanting responsively to the singer-healer who leads him. Portrayed here are mythic "Long Bodies," divinities too tall to be clothed by a single dress. These pictures, simultaneously therapeutic and religious, are visual evidence of the Navajos' high value for harmonious wholeness founded on repeating forms, a predilection manifested in the reiterated narrative symmetries of their myths. (Plate XVI, Second Dry Painting, *The Mountain Chant: A Navajo Ceremony,* Fifth Annual report of the Bureau of American Ethnology, Washington, DC, 1885, pp. 379–465.)

BLACKFOOT

This is a version of perhaps the most famous Indian myth, commonly referred to as the *"Star Husband"* story. In its Blackfoot forms it is usually cited by the name of its protagonist, Scarface, originator of the Blackfoot Sun Dance, or by that of his mother, the tragic Feather Woman. It is presented here in the form of Walter McClintock's account of a recitation to him by a Blackfoot chief, Brings-Down-the-Sun, a century ago. McClintock's description of the circumstances in which he heard the story and its effect upon him is a reminder that oral stories are always told for a definite reason to a specific audience in a quite particular situation. All the other stories in this collection were originally told in analogously unique circumstances that affected the form of the tellings – circumstances irrecoverably lost to us. McClintock's account, however, illustrates how Native American storytelling normally took place in the midst of the commonplaces of daily life, like being pestered by a dog, and emphasizes one of the myth's outstanding features, its evocation of the beauty of the physical cosmos.

That evocation begins with the girls gazing at the brilliant star, a view reversed by Feather Woman's homesick vision from the sky of her terrestrial home. Finally there is the beautified Scarface's final return to the place of the sun. The healing beneficence of the sun is invoked by the rituals of the Sun Dance, a ceremony that includes acts of self-inflicted subjective suffering recalling the irremediable sorrow of Feather Woman's longing for the beauty of her sky home. Brings-Down-the-Sun's memories of hunting and war with his father under the aegis of the gleaming planets, and his linking of their story to other legends connecting terrestrial and celestial processes is climaxed by the startling fireball crossing the Eastern sky – seen as an uncertain augury. This concatenation of mythic narratives with the celestial phenomena is disturbed by the mundane dog and the vengeful Bull Plume. But awakening in the early dawn McClintock moves

Figure 6   Blackfoot Sun Dance Story 22 is a Blackfoot account of the mythic origin of the Sun Dance, a ceremony at which many people gathered in the springtime after winter separations. But this 1877 photograph of a Blood/Blackfoot Indian shows how intensely subjective was the religious core of that ceremony. At the cost of severe physical pain, individuals manifested their personal commitment to the beneficence of the vital power of the cosmos by freely undergoing a ritual of bodily suffering.
("Indian Sun Dance," Courtesy of the Grabow Archives, Calgary, Canada.)

through the silent loveliness of the mountain landscape to behold the gleaming reality of Poia and his father, just as for untold centuries the Blackfoot had beheld them and imagined what their beauty might mean.

This conclusion is sorrowfully precious in reminding us that although Native Americans have not vanished, their world has been irrecoverably destroyed. Nowhere, even in the remotest reaches of the Rocky Mountains, will people ever again dwell as the Indians did, moving about quietly and unrestlessly amidst the vastness of an ever-changing environment scarcely touched by effects of human culture, its grandeur inspiring awe and admiration of a beauty provocative of a human imagining perhaps impossible for us today to comprehend. Yet because theirs was a self-consciousness like our own, with patience and humble attentiveness we may recover from the stories they invented something of that experience, in which is rooted the common heritage of all humankind.

22

From Walter McClintock, *The Old North Trail*. New York: Macmillan (1910), 491–503.

"There are two bright stars," Brings-Down-the-Sun said, "that sometimes rise together, just before the sun comes up, Morning Star and Young Morning Star or Star Boy (referring to the conjunction of the planets Venus and Jupiter before daybreak). I will tell you the story of these two Morning Stars, as it was related to my by my father, having been handed down to him through many generations.

"We know not when the Sun-dance had its origin. It was long ago, when the Blackfeet used dogs for beasts of burden instead of horses; when they stretched the legs and bodies of their dogs on sticks to make them large, and when they used stones instead of wooden pegs to hold down their lodges. In those days, during the moon of flowers (early summer), our people were camped near the mountains. It was a cloudless night and a warm wind blew over the prairie. Two young girls were sleeping in the long grass outside the lodge. Before daybreak, the eldest sister. So-at-sa-ki (Feather Woman), awoke. The Morning Star was just rising from the prairie. He was very beautiful, shining through the clear air of early morning. She lay gazing at this wonderful star, until he seemed very close to her, and she imagined that he was her lover. Finally she awoke her sister, exclaiming, 'Look at the Morning Star! He is beautiful and must be very wise. Many of the young men have wanted to marry me, but I love only the Morning Star.' When the leaves were turning yellow (autumn). So-at-sa-ki became very unhappy, finding herself with child. She was a pure maiden, although not knowing the father of her child. When the people discovered her secret, they taunted and ridiculed her, until she wanted to die. One day while the geese were flying southward, So-at-sa-ki went along to the river for water. As she was returning home, she beheld a young man standing before her in the trail. She modestly turned aside to pass, but he put forth his hand, as if to detain her, and she said angrily, 'Stand aside! None of the young men have ever before dared to stop me.' He replied, 'I am the Morning Star. One night, during the moon of flowers, I beheld you sleeping in the open and loved you. I have now come to ask you to return with me to the sky, to the lodge of my father, the Sun, where we will live together, and you will have no more trouble.'

"Then So-at-sa-ki remembered the night in spring, when she slept outside the lodge, and now realised that Morning Star was her husband. She saw in his hair a yellow plume, and in his hand a juniper branch with a spider web hanging from one end. He was tall and straight and his hair was long and shining. His beautiful clothes were of soft-tanned skins, and from them came a fragrance of pine and sweet grass. So-at-sa-ki replied hesitatingly, 'I must first say farewell to my father and mother.' But Morning Star allowed her to speak to no one. Fastening the feather in her hair and giving her the juniper branch to hold, he directed her to shut her eyes. She held the upper strand of the spider web in her hand and placed her feet upon the lower one. When he told her to open her eyes, she was in the sky. They were standing together before a large lodge. Morning Star said, 'This is the home of my father and mother, the Sun and the Moon,' and bade her enter. It was day-time and the Sun was away on his long journey, but the Moon was at home. Morning Star addressed his mother saying, 'One night I beheld this girl sleeping on the prairie. I loved her and she is now my wife.' The Moon welcomed So-at-sa-ki to their home. In the evening, when the Sun Chief came home, he also gladly received her. The Moon clothed So-at-sa-ki in a soft-tanned buckskin dress, trimmed with elk-teeth. She also presented her with wristlets of elk-teeth and an elk-skin robe, decorated with the sacred paint, saying, 'I give you these because you have married our son.' So-at-sa-ki lived happily in the sky with Morning Star, and learned many wonderful things. When her child was born, they called him Star Boy. The Moon then gave So-at-sa-ki a root digger, saying, 'This should be used only by pure women. You can dig all kinds of roots with it, but I warn you not to dig up the large turnip growing near the home of the Spider Man. You have now a child and it would bring unhappiness to us all.'

"Everywhere So-at-sa-ki went, she carried her baby and the root digger. She often saw the large turnip, but was afraid to touch it. One day, while passing the wonderful turnip, she thought of the mysterious warning of the Moon, and became curious to see what might be underneath. Laying her baby on the ground, she dug until her root digger stuck fast. Two large cranes came flying from the east. So-at-sa-ki besought them to help her. Thrice she called in vain, but upon the fourth call, they circled and lighted beside her. The chief crane sat upon one side of the turnip and his wife on the other. He took hold of the turnip with his long sharp bill, and moved it backwards and forwards, singing the medicine song,

'This root is sacred. Wherever I dig, my roots are sacred.'

"He repeated this song to the north, south, east and west. After the fourth song he pulled up the turnip. So-at-sa-ki looked through the hole and beheld the earth. Although she had not known it, the turnip had filled the same hole, through which Morning Star had brought her into the sky. Looking down, she saw the camp of the Blackfeet, where she had lived. She sat for a long while gazing at the old familiar scenes. The young men were playing games. The women were tanning hides and making lodges, gathering berries on the hills, and crossing the meadows to the river for water. When she turned to go home, she was crying, for she felt lonely, and longed to be back again upon the green prairies with her own people. When So-at-sa-ki arrived at the lodge, Morning Star and his mother were waiting. As soon as Morning Star looked at his wife, he exclaimed, 'You have dug up the sacred turnip!' When she did not reply, the Moon said, 'I warned you not to dig up the turnip, because I love Star Boy and do not wish to part with him.' Nothing more was said, because it was day-time and the great Sun Chief was still away on his long journey. In the evening, when he entered the lodge, he exclaimed, 'What is the matter with my daughter? She looks sad and must be in trouble.' So-at-sa-ki replied, 'Yes, I am homesick, because I have to-day looked down upon my people.' Then the Sun Chief was angry and said to Morning Star, 'If she has disobeyed, you must send her home.' The Moon interceded for So-at-sa-ki, but the Sun answered, 'She can no longer be happy with us. It is better for her to return to her own people.' Morning Star led So-at-sa-ki to the home of the Spider Man, whose web had drawn her up to the sky. He placed on her head the sacred Medicine Bonnet, which is worn only by pure women. He laid Star Boy on her breast, and wrapping them both in the elk-skin robe, bade her farewell, saying, 'We will let you down into the centre of the Indian camp and the people will behold you as you come from the sky.' The Spider Man then carefully let them down through the hole to the earth.

"It was an evening in midsummer, during the moon when the berries are ripe, when So-at-sa-ki was let down from the sky. Many of the people were outside their lodges, when suddenly they beheld a bright light in the northern sky. They saw it pass across the heavens and watched, until it sank to the ground. When the Indians reached the place, where the star had fallen, they saw a strange looking bundle. When the elk-skin cover was opened, they found a woman and her child. So-at-sa-ki was recognized by her parents. She returned to their lodge and lived with them, but never was happy. She used to go with Star Boy to the summit of a high ridge, where she sat and mourned for her husband. One night she remained alone upon the ridge. Before daybreak, when Morning Star arose from the plains, she begged him to take her back. Then he spoke to her, 'You disobeyed and therefore cannot return to the sky. Your sin is the cause of your sorrow and has brought trouble to you and your people.'

"Before So-at-sa-ki died, she told all these things to her father and mother, just as I now tell them to you. Star Boy's grandparents also died. Although born in the home of the Sun, he was very poor. He had no clothes, not even moccasins to wear. He was so timid and shy that he never played with other children. When the Blackfeet moved camp, he always followed barefoot, far behind the rest of the tribe. He feared to travel with the other people, because the other boys stoned and abused him. On his face was a mysterious scar, which became more marked as he grew older. He was ridiculed by everyone and in derision was called Poïa (Scarface).

"When Poïa became a young man, he loved a maiden of his own tribe. She was very beautiful and the daughter of a leading chief. Many of the young men wanted to marry her, but she refused them all. Poïa sent this maiden a present, with the message that he wanted to marry her, but she was proud and disdained his love. She scornfully told him, she would not accept him as her lover, until he would remove the scar from his face. Scarface was deeply grieved by the reply. He consulted with an old medicine woman, his only friend. She revealed to him, that the scar had been placed on his face by the Sun God, and that only the Sun himself could remove it. Poïa resolved to go to the home of the Sun God. The medicine woman made moccasins for him and gave him a supply of pemmican.

"Poïa journeyed alone across the plains and through the mountains, enduring many hardships and great dangers. Finally he came to the Big Water (Pacific Ocean). For three days and three nights he lay upon the shore, fasting and praying to the Sun God. On the evening of the fourth day, he beheld a bright trail leading across the water. He travelled this path until he drew near the home of the Sun, when he hid himself and waited. In the morning, the great Sun Chief came from his lodge, ready for his daily journey. He did not recognise Poïa. Angered at beholding a creature from the earth, he said to the Moon, his wife, 'I will kill him, for he comes from a good-for-nothing-race,' but she interceded and saved his life. Morning Star, their only son, a young man with a handsome face and beautifully dressed, came forth from the lodge. He brought with him dried sweet grass, which he burned as incense. He first placed Poïa in the sacred smoke, and then led him into the presence of his father and mother, the Sun and Moon. Poïa related the story of his long journey, because of his rejection by the girl he loved. Morning Star then saw how sad and worn he looked. He felt sorry for him and promised to help him.

"Poïa lived in the lodge of the Sun and Moon with Morning Star. Once, when they were hunting together, Poïa killed seven enormous birds, which had threatened the life of Morning Star. He presented four of the dead birds to the Sun and three to the Moon. The Sun rejoiced, when he knew that the dangerous birds were killed, and the Moon felt so grateful, that she besought her husband to repay him. On the intercession of Morning Star, the Sun God consented to remove the scar. He also appointed Poïa as his messenger to the Blackfeet, promising, if they would give a festival (Sun-dance) in his honor, once every year, he would restore their sick to health. He taught Poïa the secrets of the Sun-dance, and instructed him in the prayers and songs to be used. He gave him two raven feathers to wear as a sign that he came from the Sun, and a robe of soft-tanned elk-skin, with the warning that it must be worn only by a virtuous woman. She can then give the Sun-dance and the sick will recover. Morning Star gave him a magic flute and a wonderful song, with which he would be able to charm the heart of the girl he loved.

"Poïa returned to the earth and the Blackfeet camp by the Wolf Trail (Milky Way), the short path to the earth. When he had fully instructed his people concerning the Sun-dance, the Sun God took him back to the sky with the girl he loved. When Poïa returned to the home of the Sun, the Sun God made him bright and beautiful, just like his father, Morning Star. In those days Morning Star and his son could be seen together in the east. Because Poïa appears first in the sky, the Blackfeet often mistake him for his father, and he is therefore sometimes called Poks-o-piks-o-aks, Mistake Morning Star.

"I remember," continued Brings-Down-the-Sun, "when I was a young man, seeing these two bright stars rising, one after the other, before the Sun. Then, if we were going on a war, or hunting expedition, my father would awake me, saying, 'My son, I see Morning Star and Young Morning Star in the sky above the prairie. Day will soon break and it is time we were started.' For many years these stars have travelled apart. I have also seen them together in the evening sky. They went down after the sun. This summer, Morning Star and Poïa are again travelling together. I see them in the eastern sky, rising together over the prairie before dawn. Poïa comes up first. His father, Morning Star, rises soon afterwards, and then his grandfather, the Sun.

"Morning Star was given to us as a sign to herald the coming of the Sun. When he appears above the horizon, we know a new day is about to dawn. Many medicine men have dreamed of the Sun, and of the Moon, but I have never yet heard of one so powerful as to dream of Morning Star, because he shows himself in the sky for such a short time.

"The 'Star that stands still' (North Star) is different from other stars, because it never moves. All the other stars walk around it. It is a hole in the sky, the same hole through which So-at-sa-ki was first drawn up to the sky and then let down again to earth. It is the hole, through which she gazed upon the earth, after digging up the forbidden turnip. Its light is the radiance from the home of the Sun God shining through. The half circle of stars to the east (Northern Crown) is the lodge of the Spider Man, and the five bright stars just beyond (in the constellation of Hercules) are his five fingers, with which he spun the web, upon which So-at-sa-ki was let down from the sky. Whenever you see the half-buried and overgrown circles, or clusters of stones on the plains, marking the sites of Blackfeet camps in the ancient days, when they used stones to hold down the sides of their lodges, you will know why the half-circle of stars was called by our fathers, 'The Lodge of the Spider Man.'

"When So-at-sa-ki came back to earth from the lodge of the Sun, she brought with her the sacred Medicine Bonnet and dress trimmed with elk-teeth, the Turnip Digger, Sweet Grass (incense), and the Prongs for lifting hot coals from the fire. Ever since those days, these sacred articles have been used in the Sun-dance by the woman who makes the vow. The Turnip Digger is always tied to the Medicine Case, containing the Medicine Bonnet, and it now hangs from the tripod behind my lodge."

Brings-Down-the-Sun then arose saying, "The Last Brother is now pointing towards the horizon. Day will soon dawn and it is time for us to sleep." As we turned to gaze at the constellation of the Great Bear, a ball of fire suddenly appeared high in the northern sky. It flashed across the heavens, leaving in its wake a beautiful light, and burst into a shower of sparks, as it vanished in the southern sky. The Indians were filled with awe and broke out in exclamations of wonder and of fear. Some said it was a Dusty Star (Meteor), others that it was too large for a Dusty Star, which is always small and looks like a star changing its place in the sky. Those, who were filled with dread, spoke of it in subdued whispers as Is-tsi, – "The Fire"; and said it was an omen of bad luck.

Brings-Down-the-Sun had been silent. When I asked his explanation of the strange sign, he said, "The Sun God is all powerful, he watches over every one and sees everything. The Great Mystery may have sent this wonderful star as a warning, that there will be much sickness during the coming winter, or, it may be a sign that a great chief has just died. By a great chief I mean a man who had a good heart and has lived a straight life." When Brings-Down-the-Sun had finished speaking, the North Piegans quietly withdrew to their lodges.

When I lay down on my blankets, beneath the big cottonwood, the moon had risen over Lookout Butte, and was shining upon my bed, through an opening in the trees. My mind was filled with thoughts of the poetical beauty of the legends I had just heard from Brings-Down-the-Sun; of the wonderful imagination of the ancient Blackfeet medicine men who originated them; of the brilliant beauty of the night skies, which had inspired them, and of the scrupulous care with which they had been handed down from father to son.

These inspiring thoughts about the heavens were rudely interrupted by my old enemy, Kops-ksis-e, the North Piegan watch dog. He came prowling through the trees, as if in search of lurking enemies. But he was really on a thieving expedition to our camp for food, creeping stealthily along, like a moving shadow in the moonlight. When he came very suddenly and unexpectedly on my bed, covered with white canvas, he was at first startled, and stood with half-suppressed growls, but when he discovered that it belonged to the white man, whom he had, from the first, hated and distrusted, his fear quickly changed to anger. With fierce barks and bristling hair, he advanced to drive me out. Fortunately, I understood the ways of Indian dogs. If I had shown any sign of fear, he would have attacked me with a sudden rush. But I seized a big stick, and went so quickly into action, that the thoroughly frightened Kops-ksis-e gave a series of frightened yelps and fled into the forest.

Returning to my blankets, I had no sooner fallen into a light sleep, than I was again aroused, by the sound of an Indian riding furiously down the steep embankment from the plain. When I heard him enter the woods, the thought at once flashed through my mind, that it was Bull Plume, the defeated medicine man, coming to make me the victim of some vindictive purpose, before I could leave his country.[1] My bed was near a small path, a short cut from the main trail, which ran around our camp. I heard the rider coming down the trail, until he had turned into the side path, which would bring him directly to my bed. Jumping from my blankets, I hid in the thick underbrush. When his horse came to my canvas, shining in the moonlight, it reared and with a snort plunged to one side. For a moment, the rider lost his balance and swayed, as if to fall, but, quickly recovering himself, he tried to force his horse across my bed. But the frightened animal went crashing aside into the underbrush and, to my great relief, disappeared in the forest, his rider singing a Wolf song until lost in the distance.

When the moon was high, I fell asleep. It seemed but a brief interval, until I was aroused, before daybreak, by Menake and Nitana preparing our morning meal. I rolled from my warm blankets into the chill air, with a "tired feeling." I was soon refreshed by a cold bath in the river and by the fresh air of the woods in the early dawn. Taking my lariat, I hurried past the silent white lodges of the north Piegans to the hills, where our horses were feeding. Passing from the shadows of the big trees to the open prairie, I was met by a gentle breeze, coming from the mountains, fragrant with the sweet odour of wild flowers and growing grass. I climbed Lookout Butte and, from its summit, saw the shadowy forms of our horses in a meadow nearby. On the eastern horizon I beheld the two magnificent planets, Venus and Jupiter, now in conjunction. Jupiter had risen first, and I realised that he was Poïa (Scarface), and that the other planet was his father, Morning Star.

---

1 Bull Plume was a Piegan chief jealous of McClintock's friendship with Brings-Down-the-Sun because of the latter's superior prestige and knowledge of Blackfoot traditions. – KK

ONONDAGA

This tale returns us to masks, now not that of the Southwestern Tewa Laughing Warrior Girl but the origin of the Northeastern "False Faces," complexly important in many Iroquoian ceremonies.[1] This story of the evolution of a form of visual artistry is self-reflexive about the importance of storytelling. The "conclusion" of the narrative is the story told by the young hunter become old giant, the story we have just heard. It tells of his learning a marvelous art honoring the animals who are descendants of the ancestors of humans, as well as the trees of the great forests that originally covered all the Iroquoian lands. The narrative thus displays how American Indians imagined their cultures as embodying, as well as embodied in, the ever-ongoing processes of their natural environment. Terrifying "historical" giants threatening the existence of their great political confederacy become "myth giants" from whom the Indians have learned the art by which they affirm their union with the world of plants and animals. The art of carving and the art of telling of it manifest the consciousness which enables them to establish the uniqueness of their human culture as an integral element of the natural world.

This story offers a form of narrative movement that without relying on suspense is counterposed to the narrative rhetoric of repetition. The pleasure of hearing is like the pleasure of watching the flow of a river. Nothing is static – the hospitable giants become the ferocious and invulnerable destroyers, self-destroyed by the Upholder who becomes their leader to crush their stony skins and frozen hearts in an avalanche of rocks. In his

1 The League of the Iroquois, constituted of the related tribes named in the story, was one of the most powerful forces in North American politics and warfare from the mid-sixteenth century until the American Revolution.

loneliness the one escapee develops into a terrific destroyer of the natural world – only to redirect his power by transforming a young killer of animals into a patient, quiet learner of the language of the trees and of the uniquely human skill to honor with carven images the animals he had hunted. Nothing better illustrates how different the Indian conception of art is from our own than this praise of carving alone within a vast forest images in the living wood of a basswood tree, whose porous fibers welcome the sunlight entering its darkness. Indian art engages rather than separating artist and audience from the specific qualities of their sensory environment. This art sustains and makes stronger, even while it grows older, a culture that is the most complex achievement of natural life.

23

From Harriet Maxwell Converse, *Myths and Legends of the New York State Iroquois*, edited by Arthur C. Parker. Albany, NY: New York State Museum Bulletin 125 (1908), 5–195, 23–8.

Tall, fierce and hostile, they were a powerful tribe, the Stone Giants!

They invaded the country of the Iroquois during the early days of the Confederacy of the Five Nations, the Mohawks, Onondagas, Oneidas, Cayugas, and Seneca, who had sent their warriors against them only to be defeated, and they threatened the annihilation of the Confederacy.

They were feared, not because of their prodigious size, but because they were cannibals as well, and would devour men, women, and children. There is a legend of these Giants which describes them as at one time living in a peaceful state, and although powerful, gentle and hospitable in their intercourse with neighboring tribes, but from some disturbing cause they became restless, and migrated to the far northwest snow-fields, here the extreme cold of the winters "froze away their humanity," and they became "men of icy hearts."

Unable to withstand the severity of the climate, or provide themselves with sufficient food, they were again controlled by the spirit of restlessness and became wanderers, enduring all the discomforts and hardships of nomadic life, subsisting on raw meat and fish, finally drifting into cannibalism, reveling in human flesh. In the summer they would roll in the sand to harden their flesh, and their bodies became covered with scales which resisted the arrows of an enemy. For generations they had devastated nations before they swept down on the Iroquois. There they found caves to conceal themselves, from which they sallied out, destroying villages and feasting on people.

The Iroquois were being rapidly depleted, when Ta-ha-hia-wa-gon, Upholder of the Heavens, who had bestowed on them their hunting lands and fisheries, beholding their distress, determined to relieve them of the merciless invaders, came down to earth and united himself with the Stone Giants. Wonderstruck at his marvelous displays of power, they made him their chief. He brandished his club high in the air, saying, "Now we will destroy the Iroquois, make a great feast of them, and invite the Stone giants of the sky." In pretense of this intention, Sky Holder led them to a strong fort of the Onondagas, where he commanded them to hide in a deep hollow and await sunrise, when they would attack and destroy the unsuspecting people. But before dawn he scaled the high place above them and overwhelmed them with a huge mass of rocks. Only one escaped. He fled to Allegheny mountains. There he secreted himself in a cave, where he grew huge in strength and was transformed into the myth giant, Ga-nus-quah.

He was vulnerable only on the bottom of his foot, and this was not in the power of any mortal to do. Thus secure, the whole earth was his path. No human being had ever seen him. To look upon his face would be instant death. His trail in the forest could be traced by the fallen trees he had uprooted as he advanced. His footprints were impressed on the rocks where he had leaped. If a river stood in his way, he would scoop it up with his huge hands and turn it from its course. Should a mountain impede his way, with his fists he would smash a gorge through it. In the tumult of storms, his voice could be heard warning the Thunderers away from the cave of Ga-nus-quah, last of the Stone Giants.

It was the fate of a young hunter to meet this fearsome creature. During a terrific storm, the young hunter, blinded and bruised by the hail which fell like sharp flints, having lost his trail, took shelter in the hollow of a vast rock. As the darkness of night deepened, the young hunter prepared for sleep, when sud-denly the rock began to move, and from a far recess of the mountain came a strange sound. One moment it was brisk as a gurgling stream, the next gentle as the lullaby of a little brook, then burst forth in the moan of a tumbling cataract or the wail of a mad torrent – then dying away tenderly as a soft summer breeze.

Through this weird harmony the young hunter heard a deep voice. "Young warrior, beware! You are in the cave of the Stone Giant, Ga-nus-quah. Close your eyes. No human being has ever looked on me. I kill with one glance. Many have wandered into this cave, none lived to leave it. You did not come to hunt me, you came here for shelter. I will not turn you away. I will spare your life, but henceforth you must obey my commands. I will be unseen, but you will hear my voice. Unknown, I will aid you. From here you will go forth, free to live with the animals, the birds, and the fish. All these were your ancestors before you were human, and hereafter it will be your task to dedicate your life to their honoring."

"Whenever you meet one of these on your way, do not pass until you have felled a strong tree and carved its image in the wood. When you first strike the tree, if it speaks, it will be my voice, urging you to go on with your task. When trees were first set in the earth, each was given a voice. These voices you must learn, and the language of the entire forest. Now go on your way. I am watching and guiding you. Go, now, and teach mankind kindness, the brotherly goodness of all creatures who seem not to speak, and so win the way to everlasting life."

When the young hunter opened his eyes, he was standing beside a basswood tree which gradually transformed into a great mask and related to him its power.

It could see behind the sun. It could create storms, and summon the sunshine. It provoked battles or assured defeat. It knew the remedy for each disease, and could overpower Death. It knew all the poison roots and could repel their evils. Its power was life, its peace the tobacco which drowses to rest. Venomous reptiles knew its power and crept from its path. It would lead the young hunter back to his people when the Stone Giant directed. It said, "My tree, the basswood, is soft, and will transform the carver. My tree wood is porous, and the sunlight enters its darkness. The wind voice whispers to its silence and it hears. My tree wood is the life of the Go-gon-sa Mask. In all the forest there is none like it."

With this knowledge, the young hunter started on his way carving masks from the basswood trees. By the voice of the Stone Giant he was guided, and well he learned the voices of all the forest trees before he completed his tasks. In his travels he met many animals and birds, which he detained until he had carved them in the basswood. Inviting them to tarry, he learned their language and habits. Although he feared the Giant's reproofs, for constantly he heard his voice encouraging or blaming, he learned to love the descendants of his ancestors, and was sorry to leave them when ordered to return to his home.

Many years had he passed in the laborious task, and he who had entered the cave a youth had become a bent old men when, burdened with the masks he had carved, he set out on his return to his people. Year after year his burden had grown heavier, but his back broadened in strength, and he had become a giant in stature when he reached his home and told his story.

FURTHER
READING

Basso, Keith H. *Stalking with Stories and Other Essays on Western Apache Language and Culture.* Tucson: University of Arizona Press, 1990.
Highly informative on the techniques and aims of Indian storytelling.

Bierhorst, John, ed. *Four Masterworks of American Indian Literature.* Tucson: University of Arizona Press, 1974. Includes the Iroquois "Ritual of Condolence" and the Navajo "Night Chant," annotated.

Bright, William. *American Indian Linguistics and Literature.* New York: Mouton, 1984. Applies the methods of Hymes and Tedlock (see below) to Coyote stories.

Dauenhauer, Nora Marks, and Richard Dauenhauer, eds. *Haa Shuka, Our Ancestors: Tlingit Oral Narratives.* Seattle: University of Washington Press, 1987.
Sensitive translations with helpful annotations.

Fine, Elizabeth C. *The Folklore Text: from Performance to Print.* Bloomington: Indiana University Press, 1984. A survey of the methods of analysis of oral materials.

Hymes, Dell H. *"In Vain I Tried to Tell You": Essays in Native American Ethnopoetics.* Philadelphia: University of Pennsylvania Press, 1981.
An essential collection of elaborate analyses of texts, the foundation of Hymes's influence on treatment of Native American stories as works of art.

Jacobs, Melville. *The Content and Style of an Oral Literature: Clackamas Chinook Texts.* Chicago: Chicago University Press, 1959.
—— *The People Are Coming: Analyses of Clackamas Chinook Myths and Tales.* Seattle: University of Washington Press, 1960.
A detailed study of literary qualities of stories; a base for Hymes's work.

Kroeber, Karl, ed. *Traditional Literatures of the American Indian: Texts and Interpretations.* Lincoln: University of Nebraska Press, 2nd ed., 1997.
A collection of textual analyses by leading scholars of Native American storytelling.
—— *Artistry in Native American Myths.* Lincoln: University of Nebraska Press, 1998.

A description of artistic form in a wide variety of traditional Indian myths.

Kroeber, Theodora. *Ishi in Two Worlds*. Berkeley: University of California Press, 2002.

The most recent issue of a book famous since 1961, telling the story of a Yana Indian who emerged after forty years of hiding in 1911 and spent his last years in the anthropological museum in San Francisco.

Lankford, George E., ed. *Native American Legends: Southeastern Tales from the Natchez, Caddo, Biloxi, Chickasaw, and Other Nations*. Little Rock, AK: August House, 1987.

An annotated collection of stories from an area often slighted in collections.

Luthin, Herbert, ed. *Surviving Through the Days: Translation of Native California Stories*. Berkeley: University of California Press, 2002.

A large collection, carefully translated, with copious annotations.

Malotki, Ekkehart, ed. *Hopitutuwutsi/Hopi Tales: A Bilingual Collection of Hopi Indian Stories*. Flagstaff: Museum of Northern Arizona Press, 1978.

One of several such collections by Malotki.

Mattina, Anthony, ed. *The Golden Woman: The Colville Narrative of Peter J. Seymour*. Tucson: University of Arizona Press, 1985.

Focuses on a five-hour retelling of a European fairy tale, with cogent commentary.

Mihesuah, Devon A., ed. *Repatriation Reader: Who Owns American Indian Remains*. Lincoln: University of Nebraska Press, 2000.

Balanced discussions of central disputes in a major contemporary Indian–white conflict.

Mooney, James. *The Ghost-Dance Religion and Sioux Outbreak of 1890*. Lincoln: University of Nebraska Press, 1991. Reprint of the 14th Annual Report of the Bureau of American Ethnology for 1892–3, with a valuable introduction by Raymond J. DeMallie.

Ramsey, Jarrold, ed. *Coyote Was Going There: Indian Literature of the Oregon Country*. Seattle: University of Washington Press, 1977.

An excellent annotated collection.

——*Reading the Fire: Essays in the Traditional Literatures of the Far West*. Lincoln: University of Nebraska Press, 1983.

A collection of valuable essays by a literarily sensitive commentator.

Ridge, John Rollin. *The Life and Adventures of Joaquin Murietta, the Celebrated California Bandit*. Intro. Joseph Henry Jackson. Norman: University of Oklahoma Press, 1955.

In this edition of the first novel (1854) by a Native American, Jackson, besides giving Rollin's ("Yellowbird's") biography, explains the book's role in Californian historiography.

Sherzer, Joel, and Anthony C. Woodberry, eds. *Native American Discourse: Poetics and Rhetoric*. Cambridge: Cambridge University Press, 1987.

Detailed commentaries on six texts by professional linguists.

Swann, Brian, ed. *Coming to Light: Contemporary Translations of the Native American Literatures of North America*. New York: Random House, 1994.

A large anthology with useful contextualizing commentaries.

Tedlock, Dennis. *The Spoken Word and the Work of Interpretation*. Philadelphia: University of Pennsylvania Press, 1983.

A collection of seminal essays on many aspects of oral storytelling.

Thompson, Stith, ed. *Tales of the North American Indians*. Bloomington: Indiana University Press, 1966.

A famous collection of many myths, elaborately indexed and cross-referenced.

Vecsey, Christopher. *Imagine Ourselves Richly: Mythic Narratives of North American Indians*. San Francisco: Harper, 1991.

Studies of several longer myths and ceremonies.

Vizenor, Gerald, ed. *Narrative Chance: Postmodern Discourse on Native American Literatures*. Albuquerque: University of New Mexico Press, 1989.

Most notable in this excellent collection is Vizenor's essay on the Trickster.

Waldman, Carl. *Atlas of the North American Indian*. New York: Facts On File, 1985.

Fine maps and cogent text describing pre- and post-colonial migrations, wars, and social developments.

Walker, James R. *Lakota Belief and Ritual*. Ed. Raymond J. DeMallie and Elaine A. Jahner. Lincoln: University of Nebraska Press, 1980.

Valuable materials prepared by a native Lakota elder; *Lakota Myth*, edited by Jahner, also for the University of Nebraska Press (1984), is a companion volume with more stories.

Washburn, Wilcomb E. *The Indian in America*. New York: Harper, 1975.

An important study of difficulties and disasters in Indian–white relations.

Witherspoon, Gary. *Language and Art in the Navajo Universe*. Ann Arbor: University of Michigan Press, 1977.

A valuable study of the relation of language to culture.

INDEX